RANDOM HOUSE

WORLDS
NEW YORK

Published in the United States by Random House Worlds, an imprint of Random House, a division of Penguin Random House LLC, New York.

RANDOM HOUSE is a registered trademark, and RANDOM HOUSE WORLDS and colophon are trademarks of Penguin Random House LLC.

Published in hardcover in the United Kingdom by Farshore, an imprint of HarperCollins Publishers Limited.

Additional images used under license from Shutterstock.com

ISBN 978-0-593-87347-2
Ebook ISBN 978-0-593-87348-9

Printed in the United States on acid-free paper

randomhousebooks.com

2 4 6 8 9 7 5 3 1

First US Edition

Additional Illustrations by George Lee
Special thanks to Sherin Kwan, Alex Wiltshire, Jay Castello, Kelsey Ranallo and Milo Bengtsson

MINECRAFT™

BEGINNER'S GUIDE

● START YOUR SURVIVAL AND CREATIVE JOURNEYS ●

CONTENTS

HELLO!

Well, hello there! Welcome to Minecraft. If you're just starting out on an awesome new adventure, or you've been struggling to get going and want a helping hand, then you've come to the right place. You'll be surviving the night and crafting mega bases in no time!

There's so much to come to grips with in Minecraft, but don't you worry – we've gathered together a bunch of friendly guides to take you through everything you need to play your best game, whether that's in Survival or Creative mode.

SADDLE UP – YOU'RE IN FOR A WILD RIDE!

WHAT IS MINECRAFT?

Minecraft is whatever you make it! It's a world made of blocks, where you can build, mine and go on adventures. With no set story to follow, you can forge your own Journey and do whatever you want. Explore different terrains, meet new mobs around almost every corner – some friendly, some not – and build anything you can imagine. Let's dive in!

WHICH EDITION?

There are two versions of the game – Minecraft: Java Edition and Minecraft: Bedrock Edition. Both are ever so slightly different but have the same player experience. Which one you have will depend on the device you're playing on.

If you're using a mobile device or console, then you'll have Bedrock. Whereas if you're playing on a Mac or Linux, you'll have Java. The good news for Windows players is that you have the choice of either. Which one you choose may depend on whether you want to play multiplayer with your friends. Both editions allow for cross-platform play across consoles, but you'll need to have the same edition as your friends to play multiplayer with them.

SINGLE PLAYER OR MULTIPLAYER?

Do you want to play single player on your own or multiplayer with friends? Before you choose an edition, you may want to decide how you'd like to play first.

SINGLE PLAYER

Playing alone is a great way to get to know the game. There's no one there to tell you where to go and, better yet, no one to see all the silly ways you die as you come to grips with the game – and trust us, there will be some ridiculous deaths. A goat once rammed Miss Hap off a cliff (meet her on page 58)!

MULTIPLAYER

If playing with your friends is what you're after, there are ways for you to play Minecraft together. One way is to join a server – these host up to 30 people and can either be private or public. Another way is to purchase a Realm, which ten friends can safely play in. However there is a monthly fee, so you may want to split the cost with your buddies! Otherwise, you can take your device to your friend's house, join a LAN (local area network) and play together that way.

PLAYER MODES

Did you know that there are four different player modes in Minecraft? You may have heard of the most common ones – Survival and Creative – but there are also two more: Hardcore and Adventure modes. In this book, we'll be taking a look at Survival and Creative modes. Which one you choose to play first is entirely up to you!

SURVIVAL MODE

In Survival mode, you spawn with an empty inventory and have to find everything you need to live: food, tools and blocks to create shelter. With dangers lurking almost everywhere, and hunger and health bars to maintain, Survival can be tough, but that's half the fun! There is so much to do in this mode, from mining to discovering new biomes and mobs. If this sounds like the mode for you, find out more on page 22.

DIFFICULTIES

Don't let hostile mobs put you off this mode! There are four difficulty settings that you can choose between to make your game easier or harder.

NORMAL Mobs are a nuisance, but survival isn't too difficult ... if you know what you're doing!

EASY If you're looking for an easier ride, the mobs in this mode aren't as difficult to defeat.

HARD If you want more of a challenge, try Hard – all the mob stats are increased, making it harder for you to defeat them and easier for them to defeat you. In reward, the mobs may drop more valuable items.

PEACEFUL If hostile mobs just aren't for you, there's Peaceful, in which no mobs are trying to defeat you.

CREATIVE MODE

Sometimes you just want to build. If you've seen videos online of massive builds people have made, there's a good chance they've made them in Creative mode. In Creative, you don't have to collect any resources before you build – it's all just waiting for you in your inventory. If building is your main game, find out more about Creative mode on page 80.

OTHER MODES

If you're curious about the other modes, here's a quick overview: In Hardcore, if you die, it's game over – you're probably not ready for that just yet, but if you want high stakes, then this mode has them! And Adventure mode is often used to create adventure maps to tell stories – you can't break most blocks, which means you can create puzzles for your friends and they can't cheat!

FIND YOURSELF

Before you start playing, you need to choose an avatar! You can either make it look like you, or you can get creative with it. If you're impatient to start playing – we totally get it – then you can update your avatar later and start with a default skin. There are nine to choose from, so let's meet them all!

ALEX

KAI

ZURI

SUNNY

ARI

STEVE

CREATE YOUR OWN

If you want to get creative, you can customize your avatar's appearance. On a PC or Mac, you need to download a pre-existing skin online to load on the launcher window under the Skins tab. On consoles, you're able to customize your skin's features one at a time from preset lists to create an avatar that looks more like you. See what you can do on your device!

NOOR

MAKENA

EFE

GAIN CONTROL

There's a lot you can do in Minecraft, and that's reflected in the controls. You can jump, eat, dig, build, attack ... you get the idea. But don't worry, we've got you covered so that you can control your controls! And also note that on most devices, you can customize the controls to suit you. Let's take a look at what you're playing with!

MOBILE DEVICES

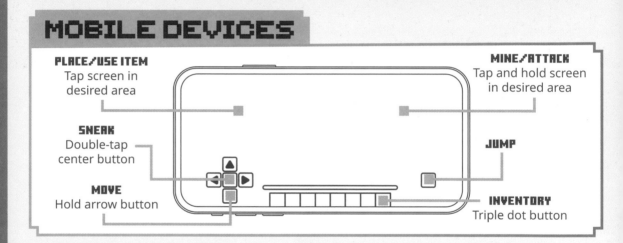

PLACE/USE ITEM
Tap screen in desired area

MINE/ATTACK
Tap and hold screen in desired area

SNEAK
Double-tap center button

JUMP

MOVE
Hold arrow button

INVENTORY
Triple dot button

NINTENDO SWITCH

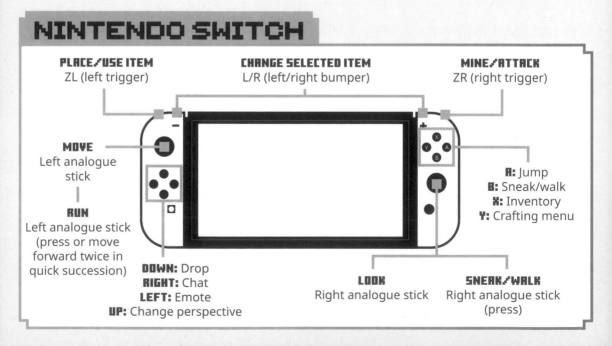

PLACE/USE ITEM
ZL (left trigger)

CHANGE SELECTED ITEM
L/R (left/right bumper)

MINE/ATTACK
ZR (right trigger)

MOVE
Left analogue stick

RUN
Left analogue stick (press or move forward twice in quick succession)

A: Jump
B: Sneak/walk
X: Inventory
Y: Crafting menu

DOWN: Drop
RIGHT: Chat
LEFT: Emote
UP: Change perspective

LOOK
Right analogue stick

SNEAK/WALK
Right analogue stick (press)

XBOX

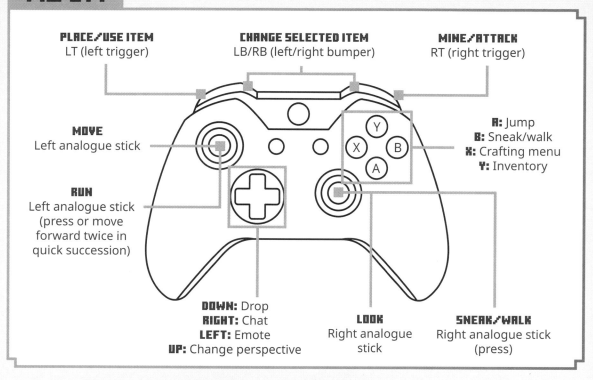

PLACE/USE ITEM
LT (left trigger)

CHANGE SELECTED ITEM
LB/RB (left/right bumper)

MINE/ATTACK
RT (right trigger)

MOVE
Left analogue stick

A: Jump
B: Sneak/walk
X: Crafting menu
Y: Inventory

RUN
Left analogue stick
(press or move
forward twice in
quick succession)

DOWN: Drop
RIGHT: Chat
LEFT: Emote
UP: Change perspective

LOOK
Right analogue
stick

SNEAK/WALK
Right analogue stick
(press)

KEYBOARD AND MOUSE

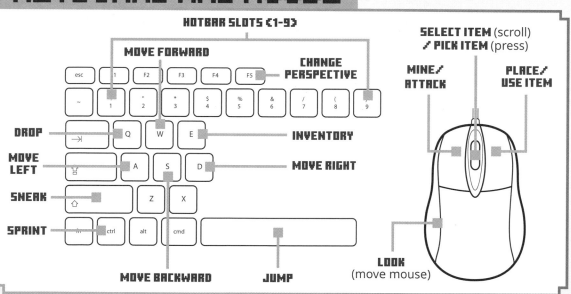

HOTBAR SLOTS (1-9)

MOVE FORWARD

CHANGE PERSPECTIVE

SELECT ITEM (scroll)
/ PICK ITEM (press)

MINE/ ATTACK

PLACE/ USE ITEM

DROP

INVENTORY

MOVE LEFT

MOVE RIGHT

SNEAK

SPRINT

MOVE BACKWARD

JUMP

LOOK
(move mouse)

HEADS UP!

Now, let's take a look at some of the things you're controlling. Your heads-up display shows you important information about your player character. In Creative mode, the most important thing will be your inventory, whereas in Survival, there's more to keep track of, such as health, hunger and experience. Let's take a look at what it all means!

CROSSHAIR

This little cross in the center of your screen is visible in all game modes. It's handy for when you're shooting ranged weapons, such as a bow or crossbow, but it's also useful for placing blocks in the correct spot.

EXPERIENCE BAR

Have you noticed those green orbs that appear after defeating mobs or completing certain tasks? The ones that look like emeralds, but never appear in your inventory? Those are experience orbs. They add to your experience level, which unlocks the ability to do things such as brew potions or enchant items.

This screen is from Survival mode.

HEALTH BAR

Your health is measured by hearts. Each heart is worth 2 health points. You have 10 hearts in total, so that's 20 health points. Try your best to keep these health points up, as running out will be fatal for you.

HOTBAR

A hotbar, you ask? What's hot about it? All the amazing stuff you put in it, of course! These 9 slots allow quick access to things in your inventory. It's always on your screen, so you can easily switch between slots.

HUNGER BAR

Luckily, you can regenerate health points by topping off your hunger bar. Like health, you have 20 hunger points, measured by 10 drumsticks. You can keep your hunger bar full by eating lots of food.

INVENTORY

Your inventory will look pretty much the same in both modes of the game, but with one notable difference: It will be empty at the beginning of your Survival journey, while you have a catalogue of things you can freely add to it in Creative mode. It will also look slightly different depending on whether you're playing Bedrock or Java edition, though it works mostly the same.

RECIPE BOOK

At the top, this lists all the items you have the materials to craft, then below you'll see everything you don't have the resources for – click on those to see recipes so you can figure out what you need to gather in order to make them.

SURVIVAL

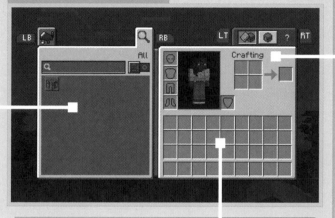

CRAFTING GRID

This 2x2 grid is where you can first craft. However, as most recipes call for a 3x3 grid, it won't be very long before you'll need to make yourself a crafting table.

STORAGE In your inventory, you have a further 27 slots. Each slot can contain up to 64 items in a stack, although some items will only stack up to 16 and some, such as weapons, won't stack at all.

ITEM CATALOGUE

In Creative, instead of a craftable section, you'll have a list of every block and item in the game. There are also fun things such as monster spawners and spawn eggs.

CREATIVE

STORAGE

Though you have the same 27 slots and hotbar as you do in Survival, when you add something to your inventory, there isn't a 64-per-slot limit – you'll have unlimited blocks and items to use!

A WHOLE NEW WORLD

By now, you're no doubt excited to dive straight in. Don't worry, you're nearly there! It's time to create your own world. In Minecraft, worlds are called seeds, and there are billions upon billions of possible seeds to explore. It's safe to say that the likelihood of you creating the same one twice is VERY rare – but not impossible!

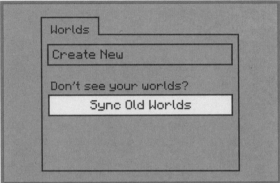

Worlds

Create New

Don't see your worlds?

Sync Old Worlds

CREATE A WORLD
Under the Worlds tab, click on Create New to begin building your new world.

GENERAL SETUP
Now, you need to come up with a name for your world. This can be anything you like! Why not get creative?

Next up, you need to decide which kind of game you want to play, and select your game mode and difficulty.

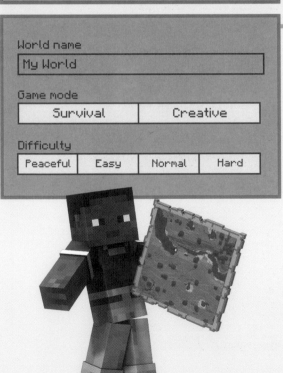

World name

My World

Game mode

| Survival | Creative |

Difficulty

| Peaceful | Easy | Normal | Hard |

ADVANCED SETUP
You can skip this bit if you're happy with a standard world.

Want to spawn the same world that your friend has? While there may be billions of seeds, you can choose to spawn a specific one. Each seed has a 19-digit code, so to spawn the same world twice, you just need this code. Of course, while the seed may be the same, it's likely you'll spawn in a different place from someone who has used the seed before.

There are some other fun adjustments you can make, such as "flat world," which will make your entire world completely flat, plus a mega handy "bonus chest" option, which will spawn you near a chest full of useful items to get you started on your journey.

SPAWNING

Where you spawn is completely random, which means that while you could spawn somewhere ideal for a beginner, you may find yourself spawning somewhere that's going to be difficult to survive. Let's take a look at the difference between a good spawn and a bad one!

LUCKY SPAWN

If you're fortunate, you'll find yourself spawning in a biome with an abundance of trees and animals, such as a taiga or savanna biome. And if you're mega lucky, you'll land near a village with plenty of resources. But even if you don't spawn in an ideal biome, as long as you start with a tree or two in sight, you can consider that a lucky spawn.

UNLUCKY SPAWN

Of course, not all spawns are lucky. There's a chance that you could spawn on a deserted island in the middle of the ocean! If that's the case, you're best off scrapping this world and spawning a new one.

BIOME, SWEET BIOME

Well done! You've created your world, now you just need to figure out where you've spawned! The Overworld is full of different landscapes, which are called biomes. As well as looking different, each one contains different resources and mobs. Take a look at the biomes on these pages to figure out where you've spawned.

TEMPERATE BIOMES

Most of these biomes are a beginner's best friend as they contain an abundance of resources to collect.

- Bamboo jungle
- Beach
- Birch forest
- Cherry grove
- Dark forest
- Flower forest
- Forest
- Jungle
- Mangrove swamp
- Meadow
- Old growth birch forest
- Plains
- Sparse jungle
- Stony peaks
- Sunflower plains
- Swamp

SNOWY BIOMES

With few food sources and the good chance of freezing in powder snow, survival will not be easy in these biomes.

- Frozen peaks
- Grove
- Ice spikes
- Jagged peaks
- Snowy beach
- Snowy plains
- Snowy slopes
- Snowy taiga

WARM BIOMES

Though sometimes harder to survive in, these biomes are full of breathtaking views and marvelous adventures.

- Badlands
- Desert
- Eroded badlands
- Savanna
- Savanna plateau
- Windswept savanna
- Wooded badlands

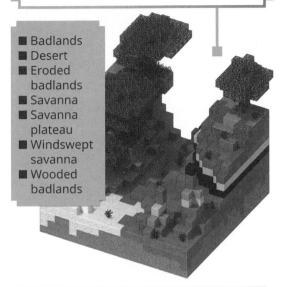

AQUATIC BIOMES

Of course, not all biomes are on land, though it's very unlikely that you'll spawn underwater.

- Cold ocean
- Deep lukewarm ocean
- Deep ocean
- Frozen ocean
- Frozen river
- Lukewarm ocean
- Mushroom fields
- Ocean
- River
- Warm ocean

COLD BIOMES

Be careful of steep drops in these biomes – they tend to be up high.

- Old growth pine taiga
- Old growth spruce taiga
- Stony shore
- Taiga
- Windswept forest
- Windswept gravelly hills
- Windswept hills

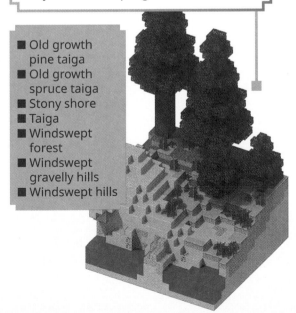

CAVE BIOMES

Some biomes exist below the surface, though you thankfully won't spawn there.

- Deep dark
- Dripstone cave
- Lush cave

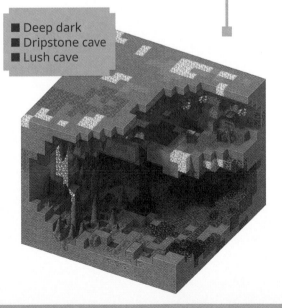

IT'S A BLOCKY WORLD, AFTER ALL

What is the first thing you think of when you hear the word "Minecraft"? Blocks, of course! If that wasn't your answer before, it will be now that you've spawned! Almost everything in Minecraft is made up of blocks, which you can mine, craft and build with. There are over 800 of them, with more being added each year. But what do you do with them?

CRAFT
You can use the blocks you collect to make all kinds of creations by using either a furnace to smelt ores or a crafting table to make items and other blocks. Most recipes for items will require multiple blocks to craft.

COLLECT
You can break blocks by hitting them with your hands, but to make it much quicker and easier, use the right tool for the job (see page 32). Once you've broken the block, you can pick it up by walking over it, and it will go into your inventory.

BUILD
Once you've collected a bunch of blocks, you can build whatever you can imagine. There are so many different blocks to collect in Minecraft that almost any building is possible if you know where to find the right materials for it.

ITEMS

If it's not a block, it's an item. There are hundreds of items ready to be crafted and found. These include everything from tools and weapons to food and flowers. Most items serve a specific purpose, which makes them incredibly useful and key to your survival.

STACKING

Unlike blocks, many items – such as weapons and tools – don't stack, while others may not let you stack up to 64. Eggs and snowballs, for instance, allow you to stack up to only 16 of them per inventory slot.

CRAFTING TABLE

To find out what you can craft with your blocks and items, open the crafting table and go to the craftable options. This will tell you what you can craft using your materials. You're sure to find many things you want in there.

FIND

There are some items that cannot be crafted and can only be found when exploring. Some you can find in chests within structures, while you'll need to defeat mobs to collect others. These include items such as saddles, tridents and leather. So if you ever find a chest, be sure to look inside!

BLOCKS

The blocks around you when you first spawn will depend on the biome you're in. Every part of the landscape that you can see is built of blocks – even the water!

WHY SURVIVAL MODE?

Survival mode is full of adventure, danger and rewards. You can steer your story in whatever direction you want. It's not surprising, then, that a lot of people start their journeys in this mode.

WHAT IS SURVIVAL MODE?

Survival is a game mode in which you must stay alive for as long as possible, gathering food to survive, resources to build and weapons to fend off hostile mobs. It can seem tricky to survive at first, but it is an incredibly rewarding way to play the game.

WHY CHOOSE SURVIVAL MODE?

DANGER

The danger of hostile mobs is half the fun of Survival mode! Sure, you might die sometimes (or a lot), but when you finally have the tools and armor to beat hostile mobs, it's extremely satisfying!

CHALLENGE

Just staying alive in Survival mode is a challenge! Not only do you need to avoid dying at the hands of a hostile mob, but you also need to ensure you tend to the basic needs of your player character: hunger and health!

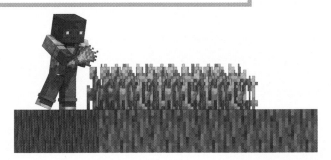

ADVENTURE

Exploring the Overworld and the other two dimensions is made that much more fun by having an empty inventory to fill with all the things you need to survive your adventures!

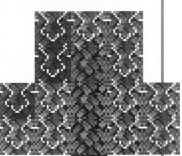

DISCOVERY

There are so many things to do in Survival mode, from learning how to farm and trade with villagers to enchanting items and defeating the Ender Dragon. What will you discover?

STORY

Everyone's Survival story is different – it's what you make it. Want to be a daring explorer? Go for it! Want to start a mining empire? Why not? The possibilities are endless!

DAY ONE

So you've taken the plunge and started your first Survival game. Now what? You've just spawned in a random biome and what to do may not be obvious. Well, now's not the time to dilly-dally – it's not long until nightfall, when hostile mobs will come out to play! Luckily for you, I, Sir Vival, am here to prepare you.

COLLECT WOOD

To collect wood without tools, you have to beat up some trees with your bare hands – don't worry, it doesn't hurt! Find any tree and start punching it until you've broken as much as you can, collecting all the logs that drop down. Then craft them into planks in your inventory.

MAKE A CRAFTING TABLE

You have four recipe slots in your inventory, which can make only basic things. Thankfully, one of those things is a crafting table, which has nine recipe slots, allowing you to craft almost every item and block you'll need.

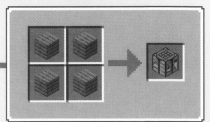

CRAFT A SWORD

Once you've got a crafting table, provided you've got enough planks left, you should be able to craft your first wooden sword. Though certainly not the strongest weapon, your wooden sword will be invaluable for defending yourself come nightfall or collecting some meat to eat. Hmm, come to think of it, maybe make some spare swords!

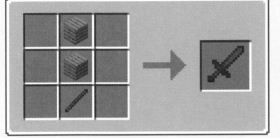

CRAFT A PICKAXE

If you've got enough planks left after you've crafted a sword, it's wise to also make yourself a wooden pickaxe or two ... or three. Sure, wooden pickaxes are fairly weak and don't last very long, but they're better than trying to collect stone with your bare hands! You'll want one for the days ahead.

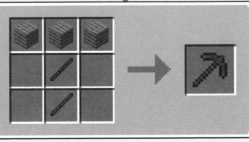

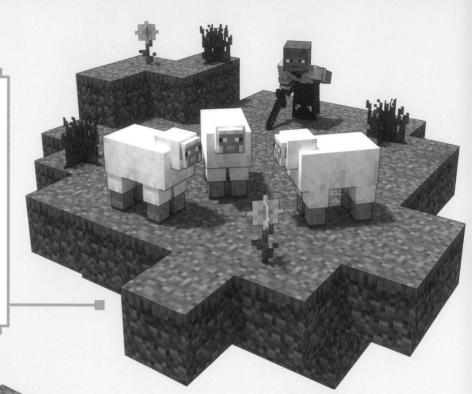

SEARCH FOR A SHEEP

Whether you find a sheep in your first day depends entirely on two things: which biome you've spawned in and luck. But if you're going to survive, you need some wool for a bed and some mutton for your belly. Follow the sounds of baaing until you find at least three sheep.

MAKE YOUR BED

If you've found yourself three of the same-colored sheep on day one, then well done! You're bossing it! With your crafting table, use your collected planks and wool to craft a bed. Clicking to use your bed will create a new respawn point, and come nightfall – provided you're not already surrounded by hostile mobs – you can sleep through the night.

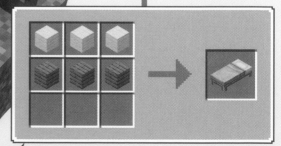

SNACK BREAK

Hostile mobs aren't the only things that can drain your health bar in Survival – hunger will do it, too! Make sure to keep a close eye on your hunger bar and have enough food to keep yourself well fed. Which biome you've spawned in will determine what food you can find. Learn more on page 46.

FIND A VILLAGE

If you manage to stumble across a village on your first day, then congrats – surviving just got a whole lot easier! Villages are full of resources for you to pillage, from beds to food. Find a villager's bed to set your spawning point, then fill your inventory with the contents of their chests and farms. Sure, you won't be making friends, but you gotta do what you gotta do!

SURVIVING YOUR FIRST NIGHT

The sun is setting, which means your first big challenge is upon you: nighttime. This is when all the hostile mobs come out to play — and defeat you. If you were lucky enough to find a village or a bed for the night, then you can skip this section. But for the rest of you, it's time to join me for a game of fight or flight.

FLIGHT

Finding a hiding spot is the best way of ensuring you survive the night. Just make sure to always put 3 blocks between you and a potential creeper – you don't want one exploding right outside! Let's take a look at some options.

CARVE A CAVERN

If you're surrounded by caves, then hiding in one might be your best bet. Find an alcove and collect enough dirt or stone to seal yourself in for the night. Leave a hole in your wall to allow you to see when the sun rises – but block it up if a skeleton starts shooting at you.

DIG A DUGOUT

Surrounded by nothing but a flat expanse? Well, what are you waiting for? Start digging! Quickly dig yourself a hole in the ground to spend the night in, and close up the entrance behind you. Occasionally remove a block from the ceiling to see if the sun has risen, then rapidly replace it – you don't want a hostile mob dropping in to say hello!

CLIMB A TREE

Are you surrounded by trees? You could climb up onto the top of one from a hilltop. Or, if you have time, build a quick staircase up to the canopy and burrow your way inside. Be sure to remove the stairs behind you, though, so the hostile mobs can't follow you up there. Then spend the night watching the stars or cozied up in the leaves and avoiding the skeletons' arrows.

BUILD A BASE

Spent your first day collecting blocks? Well, that's about to come in handy! Build a base to hide in as quickly as you can. Want to build it with planks? Great! Don't have time? Build it with dirt!

BOARD A BOAT

If you're near the ocean, then one of the best ways to survive the night is aboard a boat. With five planks, you can craft a boat. Pop it on the water and jump in. You can then spend your night exploring the coastline at a safe distance from the hostile mobs on land. Just be sure not to stop – dangers lurk beneath the waters.

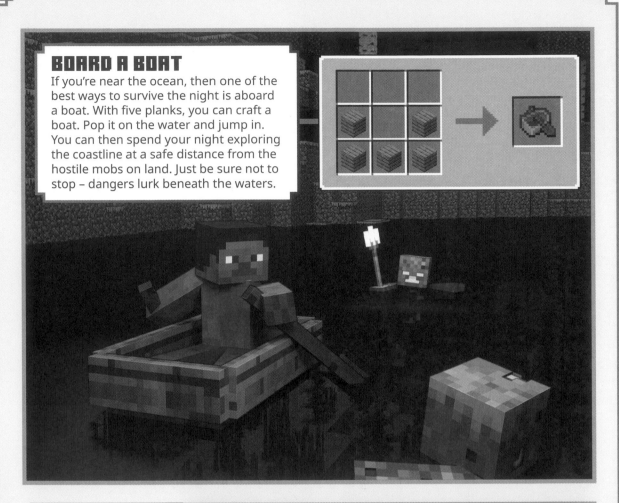

RUN

Though probably not the most foolproof strategy, sometimes running is your only option to get away from mobs such as skeletons, creepers, spiders and zombies. So long as you can actually see where you're going – not guaranteed – then there's a chance you can continuously outrun them – again, definitely not guaranteed!

FIGHT

So, you didn't manage to find a hiding spot in time, or perhaps you just love a challenge. Either way, you've found yourself outside for the night. Well, I hope you've made a sword – you're going to need it! Let's check out some defensive strategies to see you through till sunrise.

HIGH VANTAGE POINT

Find a mountain, a hill or even a mound, and climb up as high as you can. From up there, you will have the upper hand against mobs such as zombies. Pray that not many realize you're up there, and use your sword to fend off those that do. The downside? This strategy is not skeleton- or spider-proof – skeletons will shoot arrows at you from below and spiders can climb walls.

ENCLOSED SPACE

Sure, some might say you've been backed into a corner, but finding an enclosed space will at least stop mobs from approaching you from all sides. All the mobs attacking you will then (hopefully) be coming from one direction, and you can concentrate on swiping with your sword to keep them at bay. Again, those pesky skeletons might still get you with this strategy!

BUNKER DOWN

Find yourself a spot against a tree or verge, and dig down 1 block. Jump into your hole, then place that block directly above your head. This will leave a 1-block space for you to see – and fight – out of. Most mobs are at least 2 blocks tall and can't bend over, so while they're struggling to get to you, you can take swipes at their legs with your sword.

THE RIGHT TOOL FOR THE JOB

Swish! Thwack! Thunk! Don't mind me, I'm just testing out my new tools. I'm Cain Mail, by the way, tool expert and unprofessional model. While there are many items in Minecraft, tools and weapons are the most useful. Whether you're mining, battling hostile mobs or building a farm, having the right tool is key to your success.

THE TOOLS

PICKAXE Minecraft's most iconic item, the pickaxe is your go-to tool for mining ventures, and is one you'll likely use the most on your journey. It's used to mine stones, ores and metals.

AXE The axe is best used for the collection of wooden blocks, and will see you hacking down trees in no time. If you find yourself in a pinch, it can be wielded with deadly efficiency.

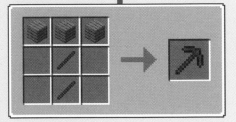

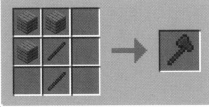

SHOVEL The best tool for digging up sand, dirt and other such soft blocks. It can also be used to create dirt path blocks from dirt and to put out campfires.

HOE Used for tilling dirt and grass blocks, transforming them into farmland, and then as a scythe for harvesting your bountiful crops. It's the perfect tool for farmers!

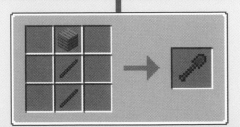

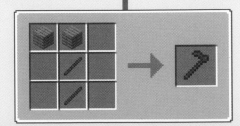

SHEARS Want wool without defeating sheep? Well then, why not give them a trim with some shears? They're also handy for other things, such as hacking down cobwebs and harvesting seeds.

FLINT AND STEEL This tool is a useful one to keep in your inventory. You never know when you might need it to light a campfire or candle, activate a Nether portal or ignite some TNT.

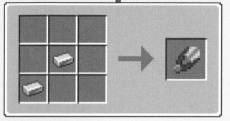

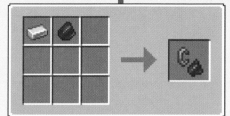

THE WEAPONS

SWORD Perfect for fending off hostile mobs and collecting meat, this is an essential tool to always have on hand. It's also surprisingly handy for mining some resources, such as cobwebs and bamboo.

BOW Enjoy beating skeletons at their own game? Then craft a bow! It may take some practice before you're as skilled as a skeleton, but being able to attack from range will be worth your while!

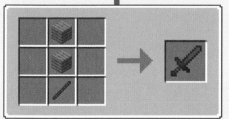

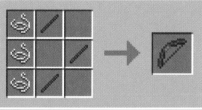

CROSSBOW This is another great weapon for ranged attacks. You need to fully draw it before you can shoot, but you'll be able to keep it loaded in your inventory.

ARROWS Your bow and crossbow won't be of much use without arrows to shoot from them! You can gather arrows dropped by defeated skeletons and craft them yourself.

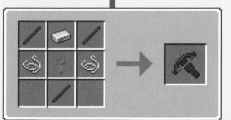

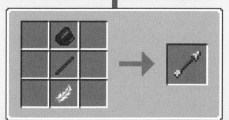

SO, YOU'VE DIED

Well, it was bound to happen eventually! Even I, Detective Sherley Holmes, get caught unawares occasionally. There are many ways you can die in Minecraft, including being defeated by mobs, falling from a great height, drowning, suffocating – you get the idea! Let's see what you can expect when it happens.

WHAT HAPPENS WHEN YOU DIE?

RESPAWNING

When you die, you will respawn where your respawn point is set to. This will either be your original spawn point or the last bed you used. Be warned – if your bed has been moved or destroyed since you last slept in it, then you'll be back where you first spawned in the game.

YOU DIED!

Steve was shot by Skeleton

Respawn

INVENTORY

It's always the way: you finally have everything you need in your inventory ... and then you die. Suddenly, you're left with nothing. But what happened to your stuff? Good news: It will be scattered right where you died. But don't dawdle! Your dropped inventory will remain there for only five minutes, then it's bye-bye, stuff! There, there, don't cry – you'll find new things.

HOW CAN I MAKE THINGS EASIER NEXT TIME?

RESPAWN POINT

If you've traveled far, then the last thing you want is to respawn right back where you started. The good news is that by placing a bed and clicking to use it, you will create a new respawn point wherever you please. So before you set out on a long adventure, be sure to pack a bed. That way, whenever night starts to fall or your survival chances are looking bleak, you can put it down and save yourself a journey.

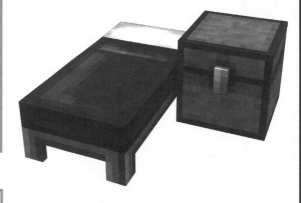

VILLAGES

Another option is to seek out villages on your journey and set respawn points on villagers' beds as you go. Finding villages isn't as easy, but it does come with the perk of providing you with more supplies for your adventure.

CHESTS

The best way to ensure you don't lose all your awesome items is to store them in chests. That way, it doesn't matter how long you spend away from your chest – your items will always be there waiting for you when you get back.

TRAVELING CHESTS

If you're planning a long journey, you're likely not going to build yourself a base every single night – you'd never get anywhere! The good news is, you can take your chests with you! You can find a donkey, mule or llama to carry them for you. You can also add chests to boats and travel with them on water.

WHO DID IT?

If you've died, there's a good chance it was because of a hostile mob. What makes them hostile? Nobody knows. But if you get too close to them, there's no stopping them from coming at you. The respawn screen tells you how you died, but don't worry if you forgot to read it, we can still work out which mob defeated you!

3 BLOCKS

2.5 BLOCKS

CREEPER

When you died, did you hear a hiss seconds before something exploded? If so, you were defeated by a creeper. Don't beat yourself up about it – this mob is mega sneaky and will creep up on you in silence with only a hiss to warn you ... seconds before it goes BOOM.

2 BLOCKS

NOT YOUR SUSPECT?

Well, you've been lucky this time, but always stay vigilant. Unlike most hostile mobs, creepers don't disappear during the day. You need to keep your eyes peeled at all times to avoid them. These mobs are best defeated from afar with a ranged weapon if you have one. If you manage to defeat one before it explodes, you could be rewarded with some gunpowder.

1.5 BLOCK

1 BLOCK

0.5 BLOCK

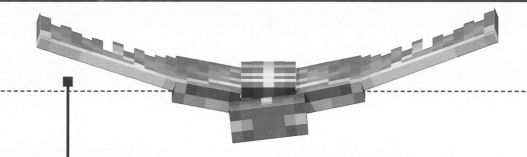

PHANTOM

Did it take you over three days to find a bed or the materials you need to make one? Did you also not die in that time ... until now? Did a blue, winged mob sweep down from the sky and attack you? If so, you've just been defeated by a phantom.

NOT YOUR SUSPECT?
Though you've avoided the phantom this time, this is a mob you don't want to face – it's unlikely you'll survive the encounter. Luckily, there is a very easy way to avoid phantom attacks: sleep. Phantoms will only attack if you've not slept or died for three consecutive days. Another way to avoid them is by getting a pet cat – phantoms don't like them!

SPIDER

Were you happily walking along with a perfectly friendly spider when suddenly it started jumping around manically and attacking you? Did the sun happen to be setting around the same time? Well, what are you still doing outside? Spiders become hostile at night!

NOT YOUR SUSPECT?
Consider yourself warned. Sure, out in the sunlight, spiders may seem perfectly friendly, but meet one in a shaded forest, in a cave or at night and you'd best be on your guard. Get out your sword and prepare to fight. There's no use in running – spiders are faster than you are. Good news: If you defeat one, it'll drop some string, which can be crafted with sticks to create a bow.

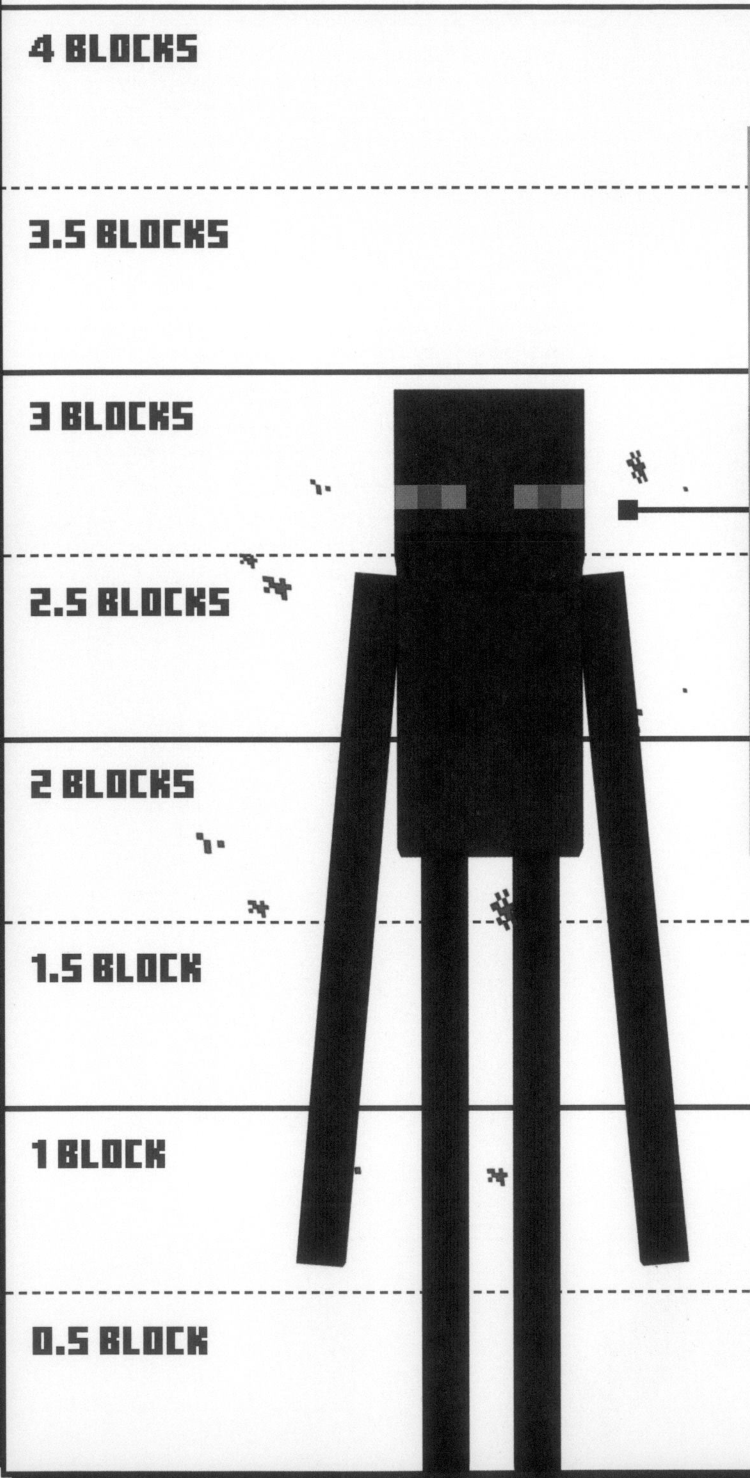

4 BLOCKS

3.5 BLOCKS

3 BLOCKS

2.5 BLOCKS

2 BLOCKS

1.5 BLOCK

1 BLOCK

0.5 BLOCK

ENDERMAN

Did you spot a rather leggy black mob nearby? Did you stare into its pinky-purple eyes? Did that mob then open its jagged mouth, shake and run straight at you or teleport to your side? Well, what did you expect for staring at it? Sheesh! You've just provoked an Enderman.

NOT YOUR SUSPECT?

Phew! Now, when you do see one, watch your manners and refrain from staring at it – it HATES that! Can't resist? Then get yourself a pumpkin helmet to mask your gaze. Too late? Well, watch out as they can teleport! If you're near water, quickly get in. Endermen hate water. You can even throw a bucket of water at it. If those aren't options, then take cover under anything 2 blocks tall – they're too tall to reach you under there, but you'll still be able to attack them.

SKELETON

Were you defeated by a bunch of arrows coming from seemingly nowhere? Did you spot a skeletal figure lurking in the darkness or shadows? Chances are, you were just defeated by a skeleton. This mob has frustratingly good aim, so if you stand still near one for too long, it'll soon turn you into a pincushion.

NOT YOUR SUSPECT?

Well, you may have dodged that arrow for now, but it won't be long until you stumble into the sight of one of these – and trust that they'll see you before you see them! Though this mob burns up in the sun, it can survive during the day by hiding in shadows. It spawns in groups, so until you've got some decent armor and ranged weapons, RUN!

WITCH

Did you just get attacked by what looked to be a pimple-nosed villager wearing a pointy hat and purple robe? Did they throw a splash potion at you with a nasty status effect? If so, you've just had your first tango with a witch. Don't be too hard on yourself, this is a wicked mob, and has all manner of potions with which to attack you and protect itself.

NOT YOUR SUSPECT?

Phew! You avoided one this time. Witches spawn in swamp huts and almost anywhere that's completely dark. They're even created when a villager gets struck by lightning! Your best bet when faced with one is to keep your distance, so they can't hit you with their potions, and attack them with a ranged weapon.

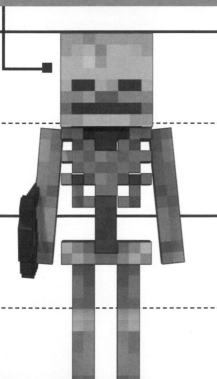

ZOMBIE

4 BLOCKS

3.5 BLOCKS

3 BLOCKS

2.5 BLOCKS

2 BLOCKS

1.5 BLOCK

1 BLOCK

0.5 BLOCK

Did you hear groans, followed by a green or brown mob in ragged clothing, holding its arms out toward you? Well then, why didn't you run when you heard the moans? Zombies (and their desert variant, husks) are slow but lethal if a group of them manages to surround you.

NOT YOUR SUSPECT?

At least now you know what to listen for. When you hear a groan, it's time to run in the opposite direction. They spawn in groups of up to four and can soon overwhelm you. If you find yourself cornered, get out your sword, swipe and then jump out of reach of their arms until you've defeated them. And no matter how hungry you are, eating their rotten flesh is not advisable!

BABY ZOMBIE

Were you attacked by something that looked like a zombie but was much smaller and MUCH faster? Better yet, was it riding a chicken? I'm afraid your defeat was probably inevitable from the moment you stumbled across this pesky mob.

NOT YOUR SUSPECT?

HIDE! Baby zombies are not only harder to outpace than their adult variant but are smaller in size, making them harder to aim at and defeat. Outrunning them will be difficult, so find a good hiding spot or climb out of their reach fast!

DROWNED

Did you stray too close to the water, only to be attacked by a mob that definitely wasn't the mermaid of your dreams? Then you've just been defeated by a drowned – an underwater zombie variant. They'll attack with their hands if you let them get close enough, or, if you're unlucky, they may be armed with a trident, which they will launch at you with deadly accuracy.

NOT YOUR SUSPECT?

Well, you've been warned. Thankfully, like zombies, they're pretty slow, so unless you've let them surround you, there's a good chance you can outrun them. If you come across one with a trident, this is pretty rare, so you might decide to take your shot at winning that awesome weapon by defeating the drowned.

ZOMBIE VILLAGER

Were you defeated by a mob that looked like a villager, only green? Well, can you take a guess at what's happened to them? They were attacked by a zombie, of course! Zombie villagers act like regular zombies, except they can be cured.

NOT YOUR SUSPECT?

That's a relief – the last thing you want is for your friendly neighborhood villager to turn against you. On the upside, there is indeed a cure! The downside? It's rare: a golden apple. But first you must inflict it with the Weakness effect by throwing a potion of Weakness at it. Not got those items on hand? Unsurprising! You're best off hiding until the sun comes up.

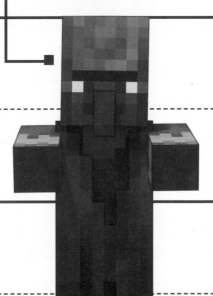

BUILDING YOUR FIRST BASE

Well, hi there! I'm Bill Ding, here to help you build your first base. You are just starting out on your adventure, so this is only a temporary space for you to take shelter in while you learn what you're doing. It won't be pretty or even very big, but there are some things to include. Let's get cracking!

OUTSIDE

You don't need to make your base huge – it just needs to be big enough to fit a few items, such as your bed, crafting table and furnace. Size 9x9 blocks are good to begin with. Choose any spot that suits you, though up on a hill is always a wise choice so that you can see hostile mobs approaching.

BLOCK CHOICES

Ideally, you want your base to be made of something sturdy such as cobblestone, but failing that, even planks and dirt will do. It doesn't need to look good!

TORCHES

To avoid mobs spawning right outside, craft some torches and place them around your build.

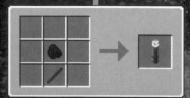

WALLS

Don't bother making the walls any taller than they need to be – you'll only spend longer collecting the materials. Build them just 3 blocks tall.

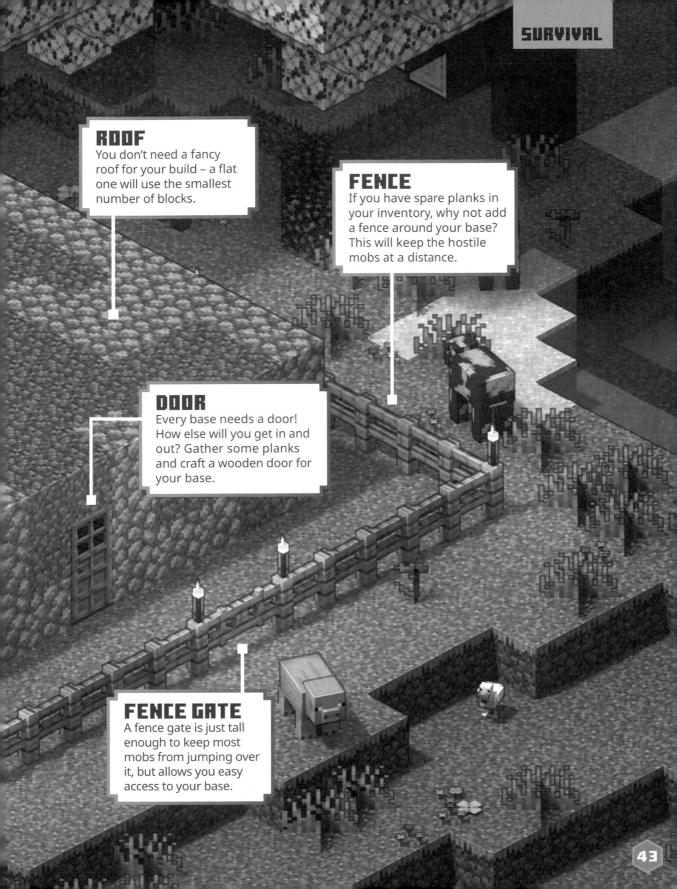

ROOF
You don't need a fancy roof for your build – a flat one will use the smallest number of blocks.

FENCE
If you have spare planks in your inventory, why not add a fence around your base? This will keep the hostile mobs at a distance.

DOOR
Every base needs a door! How else will you get in and out? Gather some planks and craft a wooden door for your base.

FENCE GATE
A fence gate is just tall enough to keep most mobs from jumping over it, but allows you easy access to your base.

INSIDE

As with the exterior, the inside of your base doesn't need to be a work of art. You don't need to decorate it with carpets, bookshelves or item frames – there will be plenty of time for that later! Just fill it with a few essentials to aid your chances of survival.

CHEST

A chest is the perfect place to store a bunch of useful items that you don't immediately need on your adventures but would hate to lose if you were to die.

FURNACE

From making charcoal for torches to cooking meat, a furnace is useful for a great many things. You're going to want one of these in your base.

CRAFTING TABLE

Before you continue on your Survival journey across the Overworld, there are plenty of things you'll want to craft first with your crafting table.

BED

Why wait inside your base all night, hiding away from hostile mobs, when you could just sleep through it and wake up when the sun rises again? A bed is essential.

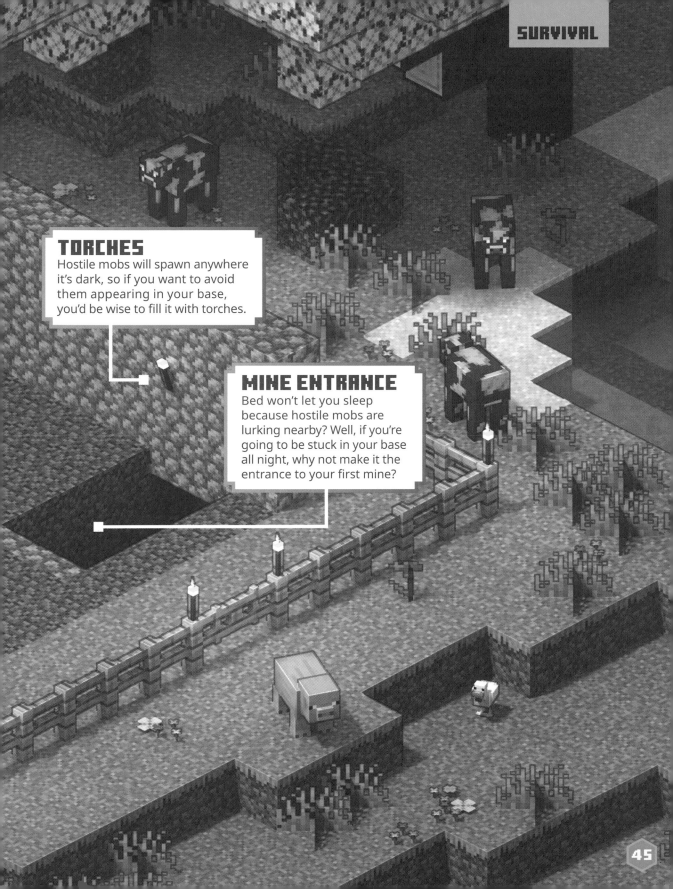

TORCHES

Hostile mobs will spawn anywhere it's dark, so if you want to avoid them appearing in your base, you'd be wise to fill it with torches.

MINE ENTRANCE

Bed won't let you sleep because hostile mobs are lurking nearby? Well, if you're going to be stuck in your base all night, why not make it the entrance to your first mine?

FOOD - WHY DO YOU NEED IT?

My, am I STARVING! I'm always hungry. What do you mean, I should stop eating raw chicken, then? Because of the Hunger effect? But I ran out of fuel to cook it with! Hi, I'm Jeff the Chef. In Survival, if you want to stay alive, you need to keep your hunger points up and be careful what you eat.

WHAT HAPPENS IF I DON'T EAT?

Well, first off, your hunger bar drains, which in turn decreases your health bar. When your health is low, it slows you down, making you vulnerable to hostile mobs. Not ideal!

ARE SOME FOODS BETTER THAN OTHERS?

Of course! Each food item is worth a different number of hunger points. For instance, cooked meat will give you more hunger points than raw meat, so always try to cook your meat first before you eat it.

WHAT ELSE CAN I USE FOOD FOR?

Certain foods can be used to breed mobs. For instance, if you feed two sheep wheat, then they'll create a baby sheep! Some foods can even be added to other ingredients to brew potions. You can also trade food with some villager professions – such as farmers and butchers – to get new items.

ARE SOME FOODS BAD FOR YOU?

Yes! Some foods will give you a nasty status effect. Poisonous potatoes and spider eyes will give you the Poison effect, while rotten flesh, pufferfish and raw chicken will give you Hunger. Though you can technically eat these items, you really shouldn't – it's not like they sound yummy, anyway!

WHERE DO I FIND FOOD?

This all comes down to the biome you're in. If you're fortunate enough to spawn in a wooded biome, such as a jungle, then food will be easy to track down, but if you find yourself in a snowy or desert biome, then getting it will be more difficult. Let's check out a few general places you can find some grub.

VILLAGES

Villager chests will almost always contain food items, such as bread and potatoes. Their farms are also great for an immediate source of food, plus seeds for starting your own farm (see page 50).

GENERATED STRUCTURES

Some generated structures contain food for you to find and collect. Woodland mansions, for instance, are a treasure trove of many items – grub included! But be warned, they are often protected by traps and hostile mobs.

HUNTING FOR MEAT

There are a lot of animal mobs in the Overworld that can be defeated for their meat to eat, such as cows, sheep, chickens, pigs and even rabbits.

GROWING IN THE WILD

There are a lot of foods, such as melons and pumpkins, that grow naturally and can be collected for food and seeds. Keep your eyes peeled, and you might just stumble across some of these wild delights!

HOW DO I EAT IT?

There's no point collecting a bunch of food if you don't know how to eat it! Just pop your food item into your inventory hotbar, select it and click to use it, then watch your hunger bar slowly fill up! It's a piece of cake!

CROPS

There are many crops for you to grow and eat in the Overworld. If you're lucky, you've spawned in a biome with crops growing in abundance for you to gather. Otherwise, finding them may be tricky and you'll have to rely on villages to provide them. Let's explore which crops are on offer!

 | 3 |

CARROT
There are a few risky ways you can get a carrot – raiding a pillager outpost or defeating a zombie, husk or zombie villager – but your safest bet is finding one in a village farm.

 | 2 |

MELON SLICE
If melon is what you're craving, then jungle biomes are your best chance, where they grow in abundance. Otherwise, you can find these in some villages and woodland mansions.

 | 4 |

APPLE
Surrounded by oak trees and in need of some food? Start hacking at oak leaves and if you're lucky, they might just drop an apple for you to eat!

 | 2 |

SWEET BERRIES
If you're in a taiga or snowy taiga biome, then you may come across some sweet berry bushes. Be wary of walking into them, though – their bushes have thorns!

 | 1 |

POTATO
You can find potatoes in all the same places as carrots, and also in villager chests. Just be wary of the poisonous potato – the clue is in the name!

 | 2 |

GLOW BERRIES
It will be a while before you find these berries – they are mainly found hanging from the ceilings of lush caves.

 | 1 |

BEETROOT
Beetroot can be used as both food and as red dye. You can find it in village farm plots.

 | 1 |

DRIED KELP
Kelp can be dried and eaten as a light snack. You can find it growing under the ocean.

WHEAT

Wheat seeds come from grass, making it the easiest crop to start farming. It's used in recipes and to breed cows, sheep, goats and mooshrooms.

COCOA BEANS

Harvested from cocoa pods in jungles, cocoa beans can be used as an ingredient in cookies and for brown dye.

MUSHROOM

A useful stew ingredient, mushrooms can be found growing in dark, shady areas or even on a strange mob called a mooshroom.

SUGAR CANE

You need this crop to make sugar for sweet recipes and you can also use it to craft paper. You'll find it growing near water edges.

PUMPKIN

You can find pumpkins growing in clusters on grass blocks in most biomes. But you will need to bake it into a pie before you can eat it.

BAMBOO

Though not edible, bamboo is a handy crop to farm. Found in jungles, it can be used both to breed pandas and to fuel furnaces.

CACTUS

Not one to eat but still useful, cacti can be found in deserts and badlands, and can be used to make green dye and to breed camels.

RECIPES

Of course, not every crop can be eaten straight away – some, such as wheat and sugar, need to be used in recipes before consumption. Here are some recipes for you to try out!

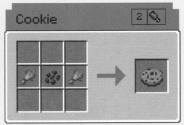

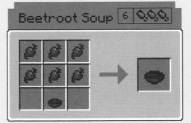

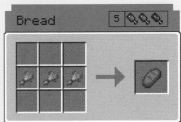

FARMING

So you want to grow your own crops? That's a great idea! Not only can you set yourself up with a steady supply of food, but crops can also be traded with villagers for other useful items such as maps and books. There are a few things to learn before you get started, so let's get you introduced to farm life!

WHAT TO PLANT

Wheat, beetroot, melons and pumpkins all have seeds that can be obtained from the crop itself and crafted within your inventory. Other crops don't need seeds and can be planted as they are. These include carrots, potatoes, sweet berries and cocoa beans.

WHERE TO PLANT

You can choose to create a farm wherever you like, but one thing is true of most crops: They must be planted within 4 blocks of water. This doesn't mean you're stuck growing next to rivers, however – just use a bucket to collect water, dig holes around your farm and pour it in.

WHICH BLOCKS TO PLANT ON

You can't just plant your crops on any block – it has to be the correct one. Most crops – such as carrots, potatoes and wheat – can be planted on farmland blocks, created by using a hoe on dirt blocks. However, some crops have different needs, such as sugar cane, which can be planted on a variety of blocks, from grass to sand.

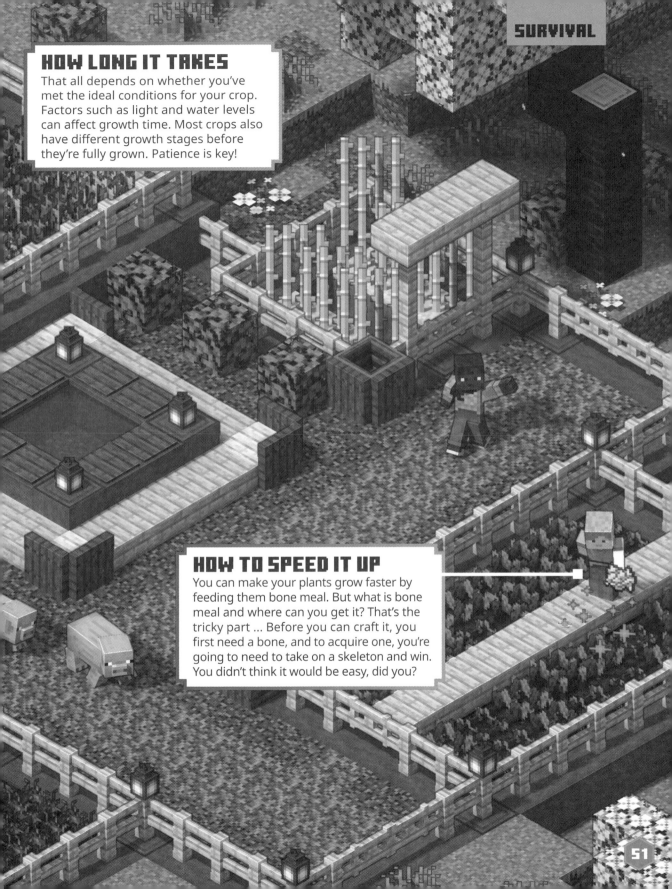

HOW LONG IT TAKES

That all depends on whether you've met the ideal conditions for your crop. Factors such as light and water levels can affect growth time. Most crops also have different growth stages before they're fully grown. Patience is key!

HOW TO SPEED IT UP

You can make your plants grow faster by feeding them bone meal. But what is bone meal and where can you get it? That's the tricky part ... Before you can craft it, you first need a bone, and to acquire one, you're going to need to take on a skeleton and win. You didn't think it would be easy, did you?

COOKING MEAT

There are no restaurants in the Overworld, so if you want to eat meat or fish, you're going to have to catch it and cook it yourself. Though you can eat most meats and fish raw, you gain many more hunger points from cooking them first. So how do you cook them? Let's find out!

FURNACE
You can craft a furnace with almost any stone block in the Overworld, making it very easy to build one. You need fuel to get its fires burning, but you can use just about anything flammable as a fuel, from coal to a crafting table. Once burning, you can cook one thing at a time until your fuel runs out.

SMOKER
You can upgrade your furnace to a smoker, which will cook your meat in half the time, though that's its only purpose – it won't smelt ores. Just like a furnace, it will need fuel to get it running, and you can use many different things. Upgraded your tools? Chuck in your old wooden ones for fuel!

CAMPFIRE
Cooking on a campfire can be either the slowest or quickest way to cook your meat. This is because, unlike the smoker and furnace, you can cook up to four items at a time. This means that while it may take longer to cook one item, you save time by cooking four at the same time. Plus it doesn't need fuel!

WHY COOK?

The evidence is in the food stats. Cooking your food will more than double the hunger points you get from your meat and fish in most cases. Why *wouldn't* you cook?

RAW MEAT	HUNGER POINTS	COOKED MEAT	HUNGER POINTS
Raw beef	3 🍖🍖	Cooked beef	8 🍖🍖🍖🍖
Raw chicken	2 🍖	Cooked chicken	6 🍖🍖🍖
Raw mutton	2 🍖	Cooked mutton	6 🍖🍖🍖
Raw rabbit	3 🍖🍖	Cooked rabbit	5 🍖🍖🍖
Raw porkchop	3 🍖🍖	Cooked porkchop	8 🍖🍖🍖🍖
Raw cod	2 🍖	Cooked cod	5 🍖🍖🍖
Raw salmon	2 🍖	Cooked salmon	6 🍖🍖🍖

FARMING ANIMALS

The good news is that you don't have to constantly chase animals for meat – you can farm them! The key to farming mobs is breeding them. For this, you need to know what foods will make them enter love mode. Let's take a look at some tips and tricks for starting up your own mob farm.

BUILD A PEN

First, you're going to want to build your mobs a pen. The easiest way to do this is by surrounding an area with wooden fences and a fence gate. This will keep your mobs in and hostile mobs out. Make sure to add some torches to light up your area – you don't want hostile mobs spawning in your pen!

GATHER SOME MOBS

You've now got a pen, but how do you get your mobs in there? This is where crops come in handy. Most mobs will follow you if you're carrying their favorite grub. Just figure out what food your chosen mob likes and then lead it into your pen.

EXPAND YOUR HERD

Now it's time to breed your animals. Most mobs can be bred by feeding two of them their favorite food, which enters them into love mode. Of course, some foods are easier to get than others. For instance, horses require a golden carrot, golden apple or enchanted golden apple – none of which is easy to find.

LIVESTOCK

Well, hello! I'm Fran Slater, a villager translator (okay, so I make it up, but shh!). There are several mobs in the Overworld that can be farmed, and all of them are passive, which means they won't attack, even if you hit them first. The villagers have all brought their mobs to auction, so let's see what's on offer. I'll translate!

SHEEP

Ewe there, take a look at my fine sheep! More than just a great source of mutton, this mob can be sheared for wool and dyed any color you want! I don't have any rare pink sheep at the moment, but if you're really lucky, you might find one in the wild.

Breed

Drops

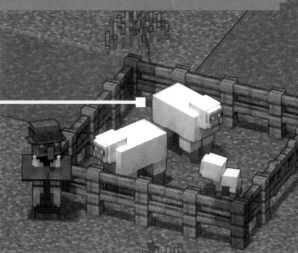

GOAT

Goats for sale! They won't give you any meat, but you can milk them – I swear your cakes will taste exactly the same! Sure, there's a small(ish) chance that they'll ram you and your friends, but look at their little beards! Don't worry, these aren't screaming goats ... but they might breed one.

Breed

Drops

PIG

Oink oink! That's pig for "Have you got a potato, carrot or beetroot in your pocket?" Not only are pigs super cute, they're a great source of porkchops, which will fill up your hunger bar in no time!

Breed

Drops

CHICKEN

Breed

Drops

Are youa keen baker? Well, take home this clucky mob today and have free eggs for life – you can't bake much without them! They'll also drop feathers, which are useful for crafting things such as arrows and quills. You can even eat the chicken's meat, but then you wouldn't have a chicken ...

MOOSHROOM

Breed

Drops

There are two types of mooshrooms – the common red-and-white variety and a rare brown variant. Not only can you milk it like a cow, but you can also use a bowl and milk it for some mushroom stew! You can even shear it to remove its mushrooms – this would make it a regular cow, though. Boring!

COW

Breed

Drops

Get your moove on and take home a friendly cow! This mob can be defeated for steak or you can grab a bucket and milk it. Milk is a main ingredient in cake, so if you've got a sweet tooth, this is the mob for you.

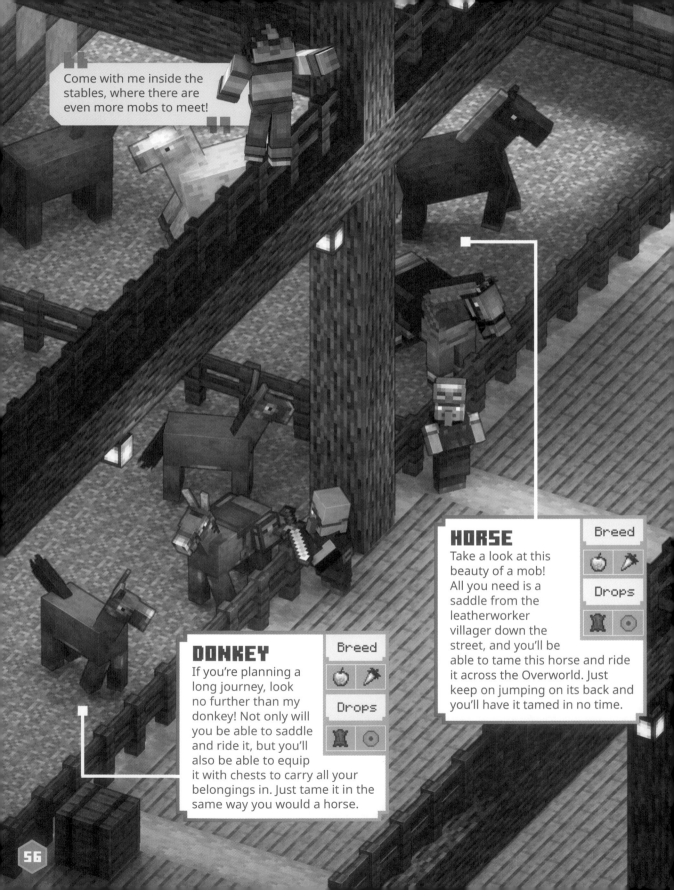

Come with me inside the stables, where there are even more mobs to meet!

HORSE

Take a look at this beauty of a mob! All you need is a saddle from the leatherworker villager down the street, and you'll be able to tame this horse and ride it across the Overworld. Just keep on jumping on its back and you'll have it tamed in no time.

Breed

Drops

DONKEY

If you're planning a long journey, look no further than my donkey! Not only will you be able to saddle and ride it, but you'll also be able to equip it with chests to carry all your belongings in. Just tame it in the same way you would a horse.

Breed

Drops

MULE

Drops

What do you get if you cross a horse and a donkey? A mule, of course! Just look how happy it is! You can guide it anywhere on a lead and, like donkeys, mules can carry chests. Unlike donkeys, you can't breed mules to create more of them.

LLAMA

Breed

Drops

We're selling mobs today? What about a llama? Not mine, of course! These mobs are loyal only to me. But perhaps another llama? Oh, wait … I don't trade llamas. You'll have to find your own in a savanna biome. They're fine companions and only spit if you attack them first. They carry all your things and you can dress them up in cute carpets!

WILDLIFE TOUR

Sorry I'm late! I'm Miss Hap, but you can call me Happy. I'm here to give you a tour of the Overworld's fascinating wildlife. Today, we'll be seeing a mixture of friendly passive mobs and neutral mobs, which could attack if provoked. Don't worry, if you follow my instructions, you'll be fine! Let's go!

FOREST

Meet Kat the cat and Ali the allay, my two faithful companions. Kat keeps creepers and phantoms at bay. I'm not sure why ... Cats clearly creep them out! Kat also brings me gifts in the mornings – not all good! You'll find cats in most villages and swamp huts. Meanwhile, you can liberate allays from woodland mansions and pillager outposts. It was mega risky saving Ali, but worth it for the stuff it gets me – I just give it an item and it finds me more!

WOLF
Wolves are neutral mobs that you can tame to be your friend. Just feed a wolf bones until it receives a red collar, and it will follow you around and chase away skeletons. Be careful not to accidentally hit one before you've tamed it, though – it has a nasty bite when provoked!

BEES
Ahh, bees, the humblest of all mobs. They're a great source of honeycombs for waxing copper and making candles and beehives, as well as honey to fill your glass bottles, which you can drink to remove Poison. But remember to light a campfire within 5 blocks under their homes before you start harvesting – you don't want a hive of angry bees after you!

DESERT

CAMEL

Score! We've found a camel! Has anyone got a saddle? These mobs can carry up to two players, at a height that most hostile mobs can't reach – handy! If that wasn't cool enough, they can dash over rivers and ravines, as well as sprint, making them by far the greatest way to get across the desert.

RABBIT

What do you mean we've run out of food? Not even a carrot to lure this little mob in? But rabbits are so hard to catch and there's nothing else to eat in the desert without finding a village! While I chase this one, let me give you some fun facts about rabbits: They spawn in almost every biome and come in a range of colors. There is also a small chance that when I finally catch this rabbit, it will drop a rabbit's foot, which is used as a potion ingredient.

JUNGLE

OCELOT

Everyone be still! Make no sudden movements. That is no ordinary cat. It's an ocelot, a rare mob that will run off if it doesn't trust you. Does anyone have some raw cod or salmon in their inventory for lunch? Good, slowly hold it out and see if it will come over. Like cats, creepers and phantoms will avoid ocelots – a handy pet indeed!

PARROT

Want to see something amazing? If I put a music disc in that jukebox, that parrot will dance for us! If you have any seeds, you can tame it. Sure, it's not as useful as my cat or allay, but it looks cute sitting on your shoulder. Just be sure not to feed it a cookie! R.I.P. Patrick the parrot.

PANDA

Quick, grab that bamboo there! Pandas will follow anyone carrying it. Fun fact about pandas: They have different personalities. They can be lazy, worried, playful, weak, aggressi— Hold up! Who hit that panda? ARGH, run! We'd have been fine if you'd left it alone!

SNOWY

POLAR BEAR

Oh, look! A family group! Let's keep our distance – the last thing we want is for the adult polar bear to think you're a danger to its cub. If you're foolish enough to attack the cub, all nearby polar bears will come to seek revenge!

FOX

Ahh, well done, you've spotted an adorable fox. If you ever see one of these pounce on a chicken, it's hysterical ... unless that was your chicken. In fact, if you keep chickens, salmon, cod, tropical fish, rabbits or even baby turtles, foxes are pretty pesky. They'll basically eat anything (except for cake) and can hold items in their mouths. Give two foxes sweet berries or glow berries to breed a kit that trusts you and will defend you against most hostile mobs.

LUSH CAVES

GLOW SQUID

I knew digging down below that azalea tree was worth it. We've found a lush cave! Do you see that glow coming from underwater? That's a glow squid! Isn't it beautiful? We're lucky to see it here – axolotls will normally attack them! When attacked, it uses its best defense: distracting mobs with its bright turquoise ink while it swims away, unseen.

BAT

Don't look up or a vampire will come down to suck your blood. Just kidding! There are no vampires in Minecraft ... yet! But there are plenty of bats in caves. These little mobs are completely harmless and fly around aimlessly – sometimes into lava. I didn't say they were clever!

AXOLOTL

Look there! It's an axolotl. This is definitely one of the cutest mobs in the Overworld – just look at its little face! If it's attacked underwater, it will play dead until it's left alone – smart, right?! You can take one of these home with you in a bucket if you like and use tropical fish to breed it.

SWAMP

FROG

Look, a frog! I told you going to a swamp would be worth the risk of witches! Oh and there's some frogspawn in the water. Good thing I brought my bucket! If you take tadpoles to a different biome, they'll grow up as different colors, depending on the biome's temperature. It will be orange if it's temperate, white if it's warm and green if it's cold. Cool, huh?

BEACH

SEA TURTLE

Before we leave, let's check out this nearby beach. Oh, look! See those sea turtles down on the sand? And there are some baby ones, too! When sea turtles grow up, they drop a scute, which you can pick up and craft into a turtle shell helmet. Oddly, if a sea turtle gets struck by lightning, it turns into a bowl!

HIT ORE MISS

Doug McDirt at your service. How ore you feeling? Ready for a mining adventure? Good! There are so many ores hidden below the surface, which can be crafted into oresome new things. The rarest ones are hidden deep below the surface, where only the most determined players will find them — are you one of them?

COPPER ORE

WHERE TO FIND IT: levels -16 to 112
BEST PLACE TO SEARCH FOR IT: dripstone cave biome
HOW TO MINE IT: stone pickaxe or stronger
WHAT TO CRAFT WITH IT: lightning rod, spyglass, brush

COAL ORE

WHERE TO FIND IT: levels 0 to 320
BEST PLACE TO SEARCH FOR IT: any biome
HOW TO MINE IT: any pickaxe
WHAT TO CRAFT WITH IT: torch, campfire, fire charge, soul torch

GOLD ORE

WHERE TO FIND IT: levels -64 to 256
BEST PLACE TO SEARCH FOR IT: badlands biome
HOW TO MINE IT: iron pickaxe or stronger
WHAT TO CRAFT WITH IT: golden apple, golden carrot, glistering melon slice, gold tools, gold armor and much more

IRON ORE

WHERE TO FIND IT: levels -64 to 320
BEST PLACE TO SEARCH FOR IT: any biome
HOW TO MINE IT: stone pickaxe or stronger
WHAT TO CRAFT WITH IT: crossbow, iron tools, iron armor, bucket, compass, flint and steel, shears and much more

LAPIS LAZULI ORE

WHERE TO FIND IT: levels -64 to 64
BEST PLACE TO SEARCH FOR IT: any biome
HOW TO MINE IT: stone pickaxe or stronger
WHAT TO CRAFT WITH IT: blue, cyan, light blue, magenta or purple dye, blue stained glass pane, blue terracotta and much more

EMERALD ORE

WHERE TO FIND IT: levels -16 to 320
BEST PLACE TO SEARCH FOR IT: mountain biome, windswept hills biome
HOW TO MINE IT: iron pickaxe or stronger
WHAT TO DO WITH IT: mostly used for trading with villagers

REDSTONE ORE

WHERE TO FIND IT: levels -64 to 15
BEST PLACE TO SEARCH FOR IT: any biome
HOW TO MINE IT: iron pickaxe or stronger
WHAT TO CRAFT WITH IT: clock, target, compass, dispenser, observer, redstone lamp, redstone torch and much more

DIAMOND ORE

WHERE TO FIND IT: levels -63 to 14
BEST PLACE TO SEARCH FOR IT: any biome
HOW TO MINE IT: iron pickaxe or stronger
WHAT TO CRAFT WITH IT: diamond tools, diamond armor, enchanting table, jukebox, smithing template and much more

The top of the ocean is at level 62 and the levels decrease as you dig down each block.

PREPARE BEFORE YOU DIG

Whoa there, hold your horses! You didn't think you could just start digging, did you? You first need to fill your inventory with the essentials. If you don't, there's a good chance you'll die by running out of food, or at the hands of hostile mobs, or by falling into lava ... You get the picture. Preparation is key.

STONE TOOLS

Before you start mining, upgrade your tools to stone. Wooden tools won't last very long underground, and the last thing you want is to get stuck when all your pickaxes break. Pack some weapons, too!

TORCHES

If you don't want mobs spawning behind you, take a large stash of torches with you, and place them as you go to keep your mine well lit. Coal is easy to find on hills or just below the surface.

BED

If you're intending to spend a while under-ground, then take a bed with you to set a new respawn point. Even the most prepared players may die, and you don't want to have to climb all the way down again.

CRAFTING TABLE

Save yourself time and take a crafting table with you. That way, you'll be able to craft whatever you need in a hurry.

STICKS

It's always handy to have a good number of sticks stored in your inventory for when you inevitably need to craft more torches or tools. Pack at least two full stacks of sticks.

FOOD

There aren't a whole lot of food sources underground – a diamond is sure to break your teeth! So make sure you pack plenty of food – mining is hungry work!

WATER BUCKET

It always helps to pack at least one water bucket. If you're lucky, you've already found one in a village chest. You can use it to put out flames if you touch lava, and to create a waterfall that you can swim up and down to scale big drops.

MINING TIPS

Of course, gear isn't all you need to prepare yourself for a mining adventure: Knowledge is power, too! Here are some of my best mining tips to keep your health bar full and your inventory stocked.

LIGHT THE WAY

Caves are huge and it's easy to get lost. Use torches to light your way like a fiery breadcrumb trail so you'll always find the exit. If you put them on the same side, you'll know which direction to head in, too. Torches will stop mobs from spawning behind you in tight tunnels, but it won't stop them from following you from elsewhere, so keep watch!

CLIMB BACK OUT

Okay, so you've made it down, but how do you get back up again? Ladders are easy to craft with sticks and will help you make the climb back up to the surface with all your new treasures.

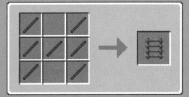

DIVE IN

Got a steep drop to get down and haven't got a water bucket yet? A lot of caves contain pools and streams. If there's one below and you're feeling brave, dive into the pool – the water will stop you from taking fall damage. But be warned: Some streams can drop you far beneath the surface if you forget to swim!

TURN UP THE VOLUME

It's not always easy to see dangers lurking around corners, so turn up your volume (or turn on your subtitles) and keep an ear/eye out for hostile mobs.

WATCH YOUR HEAD

It's never wise to mine above your head. That block above you might be stopping a heap of gravel from crashing down from above and suffocating you.

WATCH YOUR STEP

When you're near a steep drop, use the sneak function to prevent yourself from slipping off the edge.

ARE YOU FEELING CAVE?

Now you've got all your gear, you're ready to go mining, but where do you begin? Do you just start digging a hole in the middle of your base? Well, you could and you'd definitely get underground, but if you're looking for a real mining adventure, you'll want to find a cave.

WHY A CAVE?

Caves are enormous underground networks, full of perils and rewards. Exploring a cave will be much quicker than digging to get deep underground, and you'll also be able to spot ores more easily. They're full of cool sights, including lava pools (don't swim in those!), pointed dripstone and cute bats!

ARE ALL CAVES THE SAME?

Not at all! Some caves are huge and cavernous, full of underground tunnels that you can get lost in, while others are much smaller. And if you're really lucky, you might even find a lush cave, which is full of stunning greenery and the only place you'll find axolotls.

WHAT ARE THE REWARDS?

Adventure, of course! But also lots and lots of ores. You might even stumble across an abandoned mineshaft, which may contain minecarts with chests full of treasures, including diamonds, gold ingots and redstone dust. Though be warned, these structures are often inhabited by poisonous cave spiders.

WHAT ARE THE DANGERS?

Caves are pretty dark inside. And what spawns in the dark? Hostile mobs! In fact, on top of your usual darkness-loving suspects, there are silverfish, which will spring out and attack you if you mine an infested block. Then there're large drops, lava pools and the chance that you could run out of tools and get stuck down there. And don't even get me started on falling gravel! Okay, so there are quite a few dangers – but what's an adventure without a little risk?

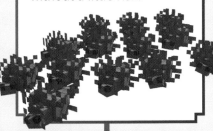

HOW DO I FIND A CAVE?

All biomes have caves hidden beneath them. Sometimes the openings will be in the sides of hills or mountains, and other times they will look like cracks in the ground. If you can't find one, you can always try to dig down – there's a good chance that you'll hit a cave eventually. To find a lush cave, try digging beneath an azalea tree in a humid biome, such as a jungle or dark forest.

" What are you waiting for? Grab your stuff and let's get mining! First one down to bedrock wins! "

ARMOR UP!

"Oh, Cain Mail, you look so good. Oh, stop it!" Don't mind me, I'm just talking to my reflection in my shiny armor. You're probably wondering how I came to look so attractive. Sure, some of it is my natural beauty, but mostly it's because of my sweet gear. No, you can't have mine – let's see how you can get your own!

HOW CAN I CRAFT IT?

You can craft armor yourself, which means there's still hope for your fashion sense. Remember those ores you gathered underground? Well, some of those can be smelted and crafted into armor. Or, if you've yet to get what you need underground, you can make armor out of leather gathered from defeating mobs such as cows, mooshrooms, horses, mules, donkeys and llamas. You can even dye it!

Iron Helmet

Iron Chestplate

Shield

Iron Leggings

Iron Boots

WHERE CAN I FIND IT?

At some point in your Minecraft journey, you'll probably think, *Where did that skeleton get that fine piece of headgear from, and how can I look that good?* No? Just me? Well, if you defeat any mob wearing armor, there's a good chance that they'll drop it. You can also trade with armorer or leatherworker villagers for it.

HOW DO I PUT IT ON?

To put on your armor, just open your inventory and drag your pieces of gear into your matching armor slots beside the stunning picture of yourself. And voilà! Just like that, you have been transformed from a drab, exposed caterpillar into a beautiful, tough-as-nails butterfly! You're welcome.

MATERIALS

But what material do you choose? Even I have to sometimes put my looks aside for practicality.

LEATHER

Though the weakest in a fight, leather will keep you from freezing in icy biomes. And the best part? You can dye it, if brown isn't your color – mine is pink!

TURTLE SHELL

Made from sea turtle scutes, this helmet will allow you to breathe underwater for an extra ten seconds! Shame there's not an entire sea turtle set ...

GOLD

Next up is gold, which, again, isn't the strongest in a fight and yellow totally isn't my color, but it will stop piglins from attacking you – at least until you give them another reason to.

CHAINMAIL

Ahh, my favorite, there's just something about it that sounds so ... me. Like me, this armor is unique. It is the only one that can't be crafted. You'll have to find – and likely fight for – this one.

IRON

Made of iron ingots, this is the easiest armor to craft for battle.

DIAMOND

This one is super tough and great in a fight. You will have to gather a lot of diamonds to get the whole set, though, so I suggest you start mining.

NETHERITE

This is the strongest material you can use and it will even protect you against fire attacks – useful if, like me, you're prone to falling into lava pools. Unfortunately, to craft it, you have to sacrifice your beautiful diamond armor to combine it with netherite ingots.

CUSTOMIZE

Want to look even more glamorous? Of course you do! There are smithing templates hidden in structures everywhere, which will allow you to transform the trims of your armor.

FINDING YOUR WAY

Hello again! Oh good, you survived our wildlife tour — that's a relief. As well as tours, I also give lessons on how to navigate the Overworld — how else do you think I find all those mobs? Getting around is the easy part. Figuring out how to get back is harder! Here are some ways that you can find your way around.

TRAVEL

Walking around the Overworld is pretty slow going and sprinting is a quick way to run out of hunger points. Thankfully, there are some much better options for you!

CAMEL

If you're in the desert and looking for a ride, this is your mob. Two players can ride it at a time, and they're also so tall that most hostile mobs can't reach you. Take that, husks! They can even dash across ravines. Take that, gravity! Oh, that one was too wide. ARGH! I'll meet you on the other siiiiiddee!

HORSE

One of the quickest ways around is on a horse. But first, you have to tame it ... *Ouch, what did you buck me off for?* See, you just have to keep on mounting it like so ... *HEY! Stop that, you're embarrassing me. Here, have a snack ...* And eventually, it will stop flinging you off its back ... Oh! I did it.

SADDLE UP

All rideable mobs need a saddle, so start searching chests in structures for one before you find a mob to ride. Or you can fish for one – I know, what monster would throw a saddle into the water?! It wasn't me drowning again and again with saddles in my inventory, I swear ...

NAVIGATE

There are a few ways to navigate the Overworld. I personally adopt the "wander around in circles" method, but I've been told that's not an effective use of time, so I will offer you some alternatives ...

LANDMARKS

To find your way back to your base, you can either build it beside a landmark, such as a hill or a river, or you can make your own. Build a stupidly high tower that can be seen for hundreds of blocks around and you'll never lose your base again!

GO TO BED

You can set a respawn point by sleeping in a bed. That way, the quickest way back there is by dying! I mean ... if you just so happen to die, you will return there. I wouldn't throw myself off a cliff to avoid walking home ... Pfft.

SUN AND MOON COMPASS

You can look at the sun and moon for your direction – they always rise in the east and set in the west, which means that you can always use their direction to find west.

DONKEY/ MULE/LLAMA

Donkeys, mules and llamas aren't as fast as horses, but do have one notable advantage: You can equip them with chests. This means you can take everything you want with you – even your feather collection!

BOAT

Traveling near an ocean or river? Boats are far quicker than swimming, plus so long as you don't stop or go too near to land, you can carry on traveling all night without hostile mobs catching you. Boats can also be equipped with chests, and you can even take a pet along for the ride!

MINECART

Do you often go the same way? Why? There's so much to explore! Oh, you want a quick way out of your mine. I see. Well then, why not build a railway? All you need are some iron ingots and sticks, and you can build a rail track to whizz along in a minecart. Okay, that does sound pretty fun.

WELCOME TO THE VILLAGE

Fran Slater here again, ready to show you around the village I've made my home! Unfortunately, most of the villagers have jobs – plus they only say "hrm" – so you're stuck with me again. I may not be the best translator, but I do know a thing or two about villages and their inhabitants that I can pass on to you.

WHERE TO FIND THEM

My village is located in a plains biome, but other villages spawn in taiga, savanna and desert biomes. Where they generate will determine the look of the buildings, the resources and the villagers' clothing.

GOSSIPS

Villagers love to gossip! If you've wronged one or treated one well, they'll all hear about it. Be nice and they'll offer you good trades. Be mean and they'll set their iron golem on you!

JOBS

Inside each building is a job site block, where employed villagers create items to trade. There are plenty of jobs to choose from, including butcher, farmer and librarian. Not every job will appear in every village and not every villager has one. Take nitwits – they do nothing at all!

FARMS

Here is our farm. Every village has one. They're full of fruits and vegetables, ripe for the picking. Quick, grab a couple. I won't tell!

RESOURCES

There are loads of resources to be found in villages besides food – there's wood, stone, maps, torches and more. Villagers are pretty laid back and will let you take these. Just make sure there's enough left for them to survive on!

BREEDING

Villagers breed on their own terms, but if you want to encourage them, then there is one way you can help: beds. Build lots of beds for them to fill! Just make sure you haven't stolen all their food as they need that to enter love mode.

PROTECTORS

Iron golems protect the village from hostile mobs. They are super loyal and will even chase off players if they get on the wrong side of too many villagers. They sometimes give the villagers a poppy as a sign of friendship.

ZOMBIE INVASION

Every now and then, a zombie slips through the villagers' defenses and turns one of them into a zombie villager. Sometimes, they even turn an entire village! If you enter a village and notice all the doors and torches are missing and it wasn't you who took them, RUN!

TREASURE AND TRAPS

Remember me? Sir Vival — I got you through your first night. Oh, you died, did you? Well, I'd say your odds are looking better for exploring the Overworld's various structures, but I'd be lying to you as most are full of booby traps and hostile mobs. At least they come with treasure — that's worth a bit of danger, isn't it?

JUNGLE TEMPLE

You're strolling through the jungle, marveling at the parrots, pandas and ocelots, when you come across a cobblestone structure. It seems abandoned, if a little unwelcoming. So what do you do? Go inside? WRONG. Without a torch and shield, this structure may as well be a giant tomb. Downstairs, there are trip wires, waiting to unleash arrows at you, and a puzzle that you're unlikely to solve in the dark.

DESERT PYRAMID

You'll probably spot this structure's terracotta patterns from a distance across the flat deserts. Inside may look empty, but don't be fooled. Hidden beneath the center is a chamber containing 4 chests full of treasures. *What's the catch*, you're wondering? Well, that would be the stone pressure plate linked to 9 TNT blocks underneath. Whatever you do, DO NOT stand on it!

PILLAGER OUTPOST

Here, you'll likely find trusty allays, trapped in cages along with iron golems. You will rescue them, won't you? Oh, you're scared of the dozens of pillagers pointing crossbows at you? That's fair enough. They are pretty scary. If you decide to take on this fight, you'll also be rewarded with plenty of loot. Just be wary of defeating the pillager captain with a banner above their head – defeating them will give you the Bad Omen effect, which will trigger a raid when you next step inside a village.

STRONGHOLD

Truth be told, the likelihood of you stumbling across this structure is very slim. For one, it's buried deep underground. You'll need to use eyes of Ender to find this structure, which requires you to risk your life in the Nether first – there will come a time when that prospect sounds appealing, I'm sure. Strongholds are full of passages and strange rooms, including an End portal room, containing the only way to the End dimension.

WOODLAND MANSION

Huge buildings filled with strange rooms and curiosities, woodland mansions are a treasure trove for explorers. But of course, those treasures are not left undefended. Evokers and vindicators guard this structure, and you can be sure they won't be too happy to discover thieves in their midst! Keep an eye out for another allay trapped within.

NEW DIMENSIONS

So you now know a fair amount about the Overworld, Minecraft's friendliest dimension. But what about the other two? I'm Nellie Porter, and I'm here to let you know that there are scarier things out there than a creeper! If you thought the Overworld was full of dangers, you've not seen anything yet!

THE NETHER

The first new dimension you'll discover is the Nether. It's full of alien landscapes and terrifying mobs, so you'll want to have mastered your battle skills before you step foot here – you will have to fight to survive.

HOW DO I GET THERE?

To get to the Nether, you need to travel by Nether portal. You can either build one yourself with 10 blocks of obsidian, or you may stumble across one in the Overworld that can be fixed. But first you need a diamond pickaxe – the only tool that will mine obsidian. Once built, ignite the portal with fire and off you go! That was the easy part ...

WHAT CAN I EXPECT WHEN I GET THERE?

As far as dimensions go, this one is pretty dangerous. Full of lava pits, steep drops and hostile mobs, death comes pretty easily. In fact, there is only one passive mob in the entire Nether. Plus there's only one food source – and hoglins aren't defeated easily!

WHY WOULD I EVER WISH TO GO THERE?

A challenge? Adventure? Loads of treasure? The hope to one day see the End, too? Take your pick! The Nether has just as many treasures as it does risks. Also, if you ever want to brew potions, you're going to want to defeat a blaze for your brewing stand.

THE END

The other dimension to explore is the End, home to the Ender Dragon – one of Minecraft's mightiest hostile mobs. Getting here isn't straightforward, but surviving it sure is an achievement to boast about!

HOW DO I GET THERE?

Getting here is a little (okay, VERY) tricky. You first need to find a stronghold, which contains an End portal. However, they are deep underground, and locating one requires an eye of Ender. To craft an eye of Ender, you need two ingredients: Ender pearls and blaze powder. The first of these is obtained by defeating Endermen and the second by defeating blazes in the Nether – yikes! Once you've found a stronghold and located the End portal room, you then need more Ender pearls to activate the End portal. Good luck!

WHAT CAN I EXPECT WHEN I GET THERE?

Upon arriving in the End, you'll be greeted by the Ender Dragon. No, this is not a friendly dragon – if only! Instead, you'll need to engage in your biggest boss battle yet. And if you think you can duck out, you'll be sorely disappointed. The only way to leave the End once you've entered it is by defeating the Ender Dragon or being defeated yourself. Armor up!

WHY WOULD I EVER WISH TO GO THERE?

Okay, so everything I've told you so far sounds pretty scary. And it is. You shouldn't go to the End unless you're prepared for a fight. But the battle is half the fun! One day, you'll be dying for a challenge like this – literally! Plus once you defeat the Ender Dragon, you'll be able to visit End cities, which are full of awesome loot, including elytra: wings that will allow you to fly!

WHY CREATIVE MODE?

If you're looking to build to your heart's content without the fear of hostile mobs and the challenge of having to collect all the blocks first, then this is your mode.

WHAT IS CREATIVE MODE?

Just as you play to survive in Survival mode, in Creative mode you play to create. With every block available in your inventory – including building blocks, TNT and even mob spawners – the only limit is your imagination. Want to build an animal sanctuary? Go for it! Want to build a top-secret underground lair? The Overworld is your oyster!

WHY CHOOSE CREATIVE MODE?

NO LIMITS

In Creative mode, you have access to unlimited blocks, all ready in your inventory. And unlike in Survival mode, you don't need to travel to another dimension to get the blocks from it. You can build with whatever you like! Just open your inventory and take your pick.

SPEED

Not having to collect or craft blocks is a massive bonus. If you want to build a giant glass castle, then you can do so, without needing to first find a bunch of sand to smelt into glass. Just pop a block into your hotbar and it will never run out.

NO HOSTILE MOBS

Fed up with being defeated every time the sun goes down? In Creative mode, not only can you choose for the sun to not go down at all, but you don't have to play in fear of hostile mobs at your back – they leave you alone!

YOU CAN FLY

You don't need to travel to the End to find elytra to soar. Just double jump and you'll be up, up and away! This makes it much easier to find the perfect spot to build or to create huge structures, without the need to climb the walls.

NO HUNGER

Build and build for hours without the fear of starvation in Creative mode. Just think of what you could create and how many pigs you'll save without the need to stop for emergency snack breaks!

PICK A SPOT

The first decision you are faced with is "Where do I build?" With so many biomes to choose from, it's a difficult question, for sure. Well, you're in luck as I, Anne Scape, just so happen to be an expert in landscapes – well, I like looking at them. That counts, right? Let's find the perfect spot!

SAND-SCAPE

For some fun in the sun, why not hunt for a nice spot in a desert biome? You could build a giant sandcastle or find a flat spot to build an enormous pyramid. The possibilities are endless!

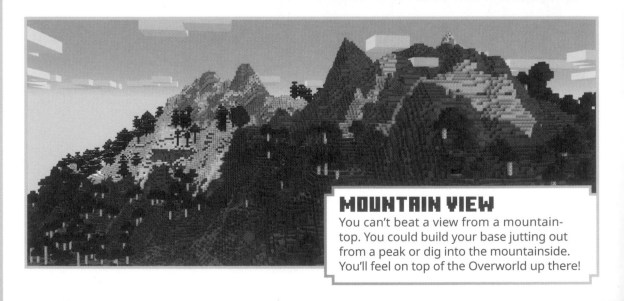

MOUNTAIN VIEW

You can't beat a view from a mountain-top. You could build your base jutting out from a peak or dig into the mountainside. You'll feel on top of the Overworld up there!

WINTER WONDERLAND

Wrap up warm and head on over to a snowy biome to build a super-cool base. These biomes are perfect for a cozy chalet, igloo or ice castle.

UNDERWATER KINGDOM

What's a major perk of Creative mode? Breathing underwater, of course! That's right: You can make your mermaid dreams come true and live under the ocean.

> Don't waste time walking to all these biomes – double jump and soar through the air!

WOODLAND CLEARING

Who wouldn't want to build a log cabin in this dreamy clearing in a wooded biome? If you need more space, simply remove a few trees and level out the ground.

FROM THE GROUND UP

Now that you've found the perfect spot, I'm back to help you build a base. Oh, you don't remember me? I'm Bill, duh! The famous Minecraft architect! What do you mean you haven't heard of me? That hurts. Well, soon I'm sure you'll be telling all your friends about me. That's Bill Ding, okay? With two Ls.

BUILDING BLOCKS

Before you start, you need to decide which blocks to use. There are so many to choose from that knowing where to start can be daunting. I suggest you begin by picking just a few different blocks to create a look. For instance, this build uses just these blocks and items:

OAK LOG

COBBLESTONE

OAK DOOR

TORCH

GLASS PANE

OAK SLAB

STEP 1

Start by building 6 pillars, 3 oak logs tall, in a 7x9 block rectangle with 3 pillars evenly spaced out down each long side. Carve out the space between the lines of pillars and replace the floor with oak slabs, adding one extra slab at the front of your build, where your door will be.

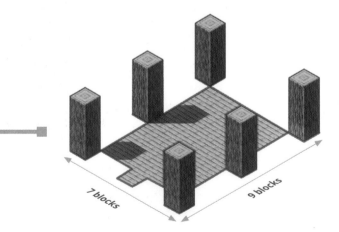

7 blocks

9 blocks

STEP 2

Use cobblestone blocks to fill in the walls between your pillars, leaving a 2-block-tall space for a door at the front and some holes for windows on the sides. Place an extra 3 cobblestone blocks on top of the walls at the front and back of the house.

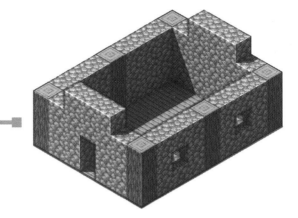

STEP 3

Add an oak door to the front of your house and glass panes in the window spaces. Then place some torches to light up your build, both inside and out.

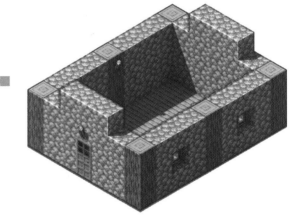

STEP 4

Finally, it's time for the trickiest bit: the roof. Start by adding a lip of oak slabs around the top layer of walls on the long sides of the build, wrapping around 1 block at the front and back. Then in 2-block overlapping layers, build your roof up to meet in the middle.

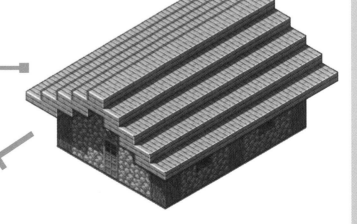

FRONT

FINISHING TOUCHES

Well done, you've built your first base in Creative mode, but the fun doesn't end there! Now it's time to decorate. You'll need to get crafty to outfit your home as there aren't many furniture items in your inventory. Let's take a look at how to craft some basic pieces that you can tweak and customize.

CHAIRS

There aren't functional chairs in the game, but that doesn't stop you from faking some! Using slabs, doors, stairs and trapdoors, you can make all kinds of chairs.

TABLES

Tables can be built with a range of unlikely blocks, including stairs, slabs, trapdoors, fences, carpets and even anvils!

ENCHANTING STATION

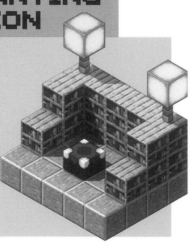

Using bookshelves, you can build the perfect enchanting station. Or leave out the enchanting table to build a library, and fill it with epic stories.

STORAGE

If, like me, you're a lover of organization, why not make this wall of chests, complete with signs to tell you what's in each one, and a ladder to reach them all!

BEDS

Beds don't need to be boring, even if they are supposed to send you to sleep. You can use slabs, trapdoors, planks and crafting tables to jazz them up.

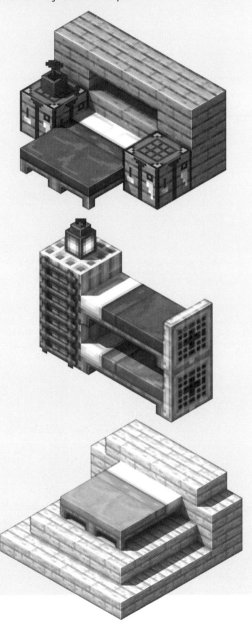

RUGS

Rugs are a great way to add character to your builds. Just use different colored carpets to make a pattern.

POTION STATION

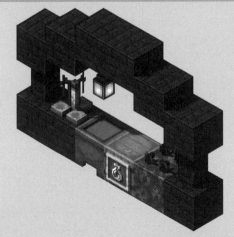

Who needs a kitchen when you can have a potion station? I used slabs, blocks and walls to create a frame and added a soul lantern.

GREEN FINGERS

You didn't think you were finished, did you? There're HEAPS more character you can add outside! Your inventory contains plenty of trees, leaves and flowers to add to your garden, and that's just the plants. There're loads of things you can build to create a truly awesome outdoor space. Let's take a look at some ideas!

PLANTERS

You can either use an ancient pot or trapdoors around a dirt block to create a planter, then add fences and leaves to make trees and bushes. What could be cuter than a tiny tree in a pot?

LIGHTING

Sure, torches and lanterns look pretty good already, but are you really going to settle for something so simple? Of course not! Use walls, fences, trapdoors and slabs to create lighting that's unique.

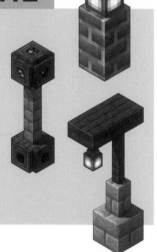

SWING SEAT

Who doesn't love a garden swing? Add some logs to a tree to create a branch, then use chains attached to slabs to build a swing for your garden. Use trapdoors to give the seat a back.

WELL

It is my wish that you build this well! Use a mixture of blocks, slabs, walls and fences to create the structure, then add a water source block and a chain.

FOUNTAIN

First build a patterned patio and statue. Then use stairs to create a pool and add a water source on top of your statue to make a fountain.

BRIDGES

Don't be afraid to get creative with bridges. You can build a traditional hump bridge, or go for something more rustic, such as one made out of campfires. Just be sure to extinguish them before you cross!

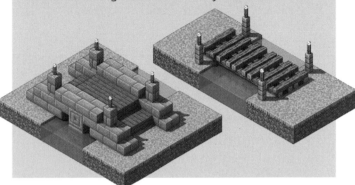

PATHS AND ROADS

You can add character with the blocks you use for the paths and roads connecting your builds, just like this road made of blackstone and bone blocks, or this mixed-stone pathway.

POND

Build a pond for resident frogs to take a dip in. Just dig an uneven circle, fill it with water and add some lily pads, then surround it with other plants and blocks.

Take a look at how you can combine these builds to create a fun outdoor space on page 92!

BUILD IDEAS

Here are just some of the structures I've built – do you see why I'm famous now? No? Well, I challenge you to do better! Once you've built your first base, there are endless ways you can adapt it to make something new. See for yourself! These are all variations of our original build.

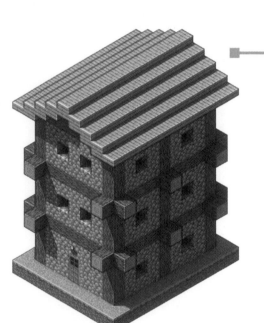

APARTMENTS
Elevate your base by turning it into a block of apartments. Repeat your base again and again to create the floors. Just remember to add stairs!

SHOP
Want to set up shop? Add an awning, big windows and some lecterns, and you've got yourself an adorable shopfront!

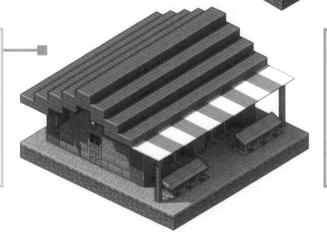

JAIL
Hostile mobs won't defeat you in this mode, but you could always throw them into jail if they annoy you! Just add some iron bars to your build and flatten the roof.

A SPLASH OF COLOR

Here are just some of the blocks you can use to add color to your builds. Why not try introducing them into your next base?

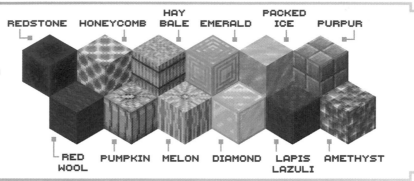

REDSTONE HONEYCOMB HAY BALE EMERALD PACKED ICE PURPUR

RED WOOL PUMPKIN MELON DIAMOND LAPIS LAZULI AMETHYST

BARN

This one is for the fellow mob-lovers out there! Remove your door and add in some fences to give your favorite mobs a home.

LIBRARY

With not one, but TWO types of bookshelves in your inventory, why *wouldn't* you want to build yourself a library?

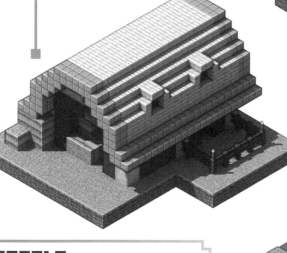

CASTLE

Want a base fit for a king and queen? Add some battlements along the top and trapdoors around your doorway to make it look regal!

BUILDING A VILLAGE

Now you know how to build all kinds of different structures, why not put them together to create your very own village? You could make an entire street of different shops, a village square, cute terraced houses, some apartments, a farm – anything you like. The possibilities are endless! Have fun being creative!

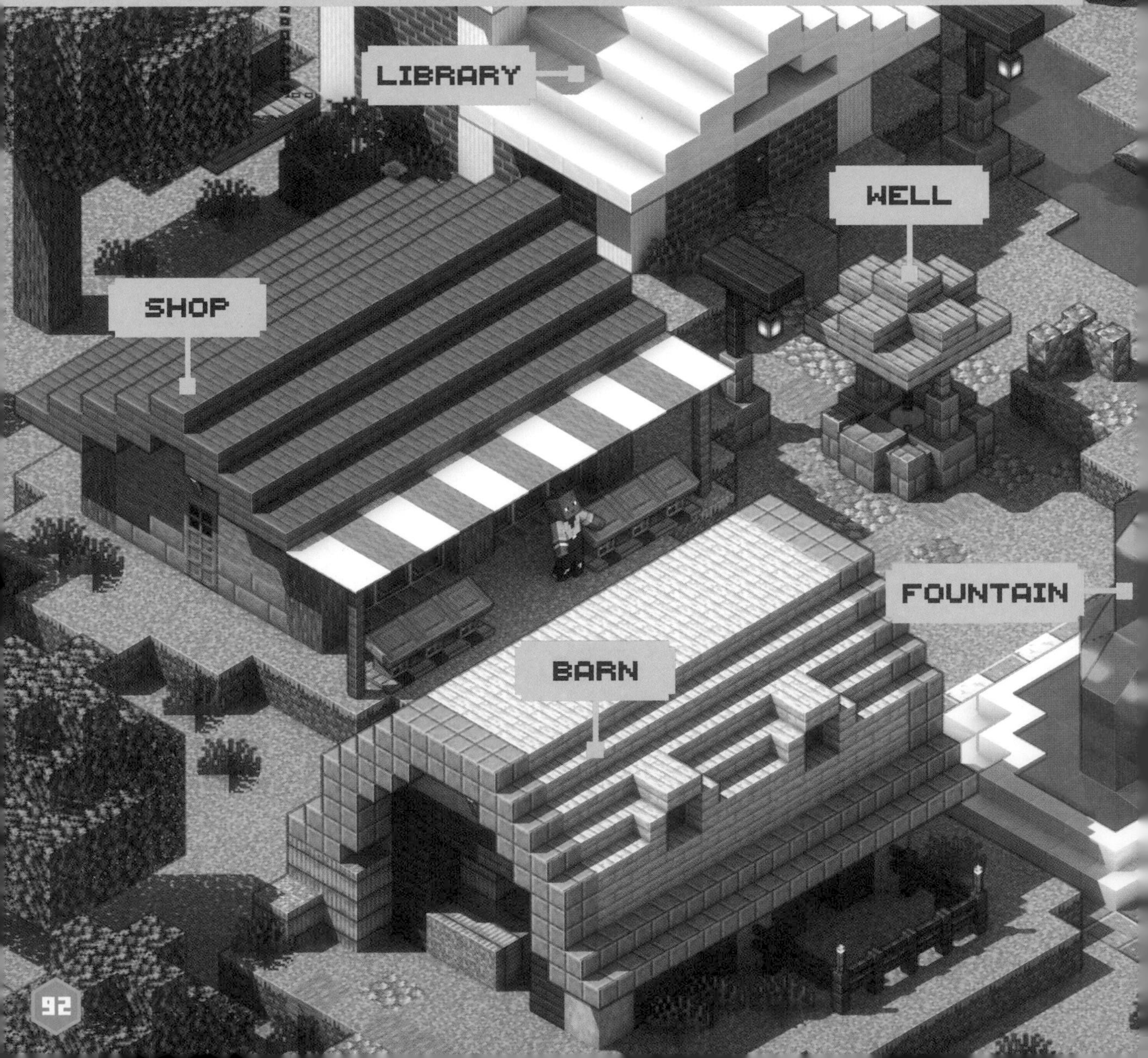

LIBRARY

WELL

SHOP

FOUNTAIN

BARN

POND

CASTLE

JAIL

CREATIVE

PATHS

APARTMENTS

BRIDGE

STREET LAMP

GOODBYE

Well, that's it! You're now armed with all the tools you need to begin your epic adventure in Minecraft. Are you excited? We're definitely excited for you!

Where will you start first? Will you battle off hordes of mobs in Survival mode or will you build an incredible structure in Creative?

Whatever your journey, we hope you have the best time learning and discovering these enormous and thrilling worlds.

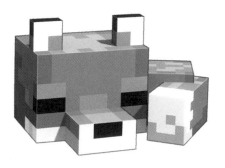